The Poems of Abu Sa'

The Poems of Abu Sa'id Abu'l Kheyr

Translated into English
with the original Persian
and an Introduction by
Reza Ordoubadian

**Ibex Publishers,
Bethesda, Maryland**

The Poems of Abu Sa'id Abu'l Kheyr
Bilingual English and Persian Edition

Introduction and English Translation by Reza Ordoubadian

Cover photograph: dome of Lotfollah Mosque, Isfahan courtesy of seier+seier+seier.

ISBN-10: 1-58814-039-3
ISBN-13: 978-1-58814-039-5 ·

Manufactured in Canada

The paper used in this book meets the minimum requirements of the American National Standard for Information Services—Permanence of Paper for Printed Library Materials, ANSI Z39.48–1984

This book was printed on 100 percent recycled paper.

Ibex Publishers strives to create books which are complete and free of error. Please help us with future editions by reporting any errors or suggestions for improvement to the address below or: corrections@ibexpub.com

Ibex Publishers, Inc.
Post Office Box 30087
Bethesda, Maryland 20824
Telephone: 301–718–8188
Facsimile: 301–907–8707
www.ibexpublishers.com

LIBRARY OF CONGRESS CATALOGING-IN-PUBLICATION INFORMATION

Abu Sa'id ibn Abi al-Khayr, 967-1049.
[Poems. English & Persian]
The poems of Abu Sa'id Abu'l Kheyr / translated into English with the original Persian and an introduction by Reza Ordoubadian. — Bilingual English and Persian ed.
p. cm. — (Classics of Persian literature ; 8)
Includes bibliographical references and index.
ISBN 978-1-58814-039-5 (alk. paper)
1. Abu Sa'id ibn Abi al-Khayr, 967-1049—Translations into English.   2. Sufi poetry, Persian—Translations into English.   I. Ordoubadian, Reza.   II. Title.
PK6451.A28A2   2009
891'.5511—dc22   2009006104

to
Margaret Ordoubadian
and
Björn Ordoubadian

Table of Contents

Introduction[1]

Abu Sa'id is sitting squat on a cushion in a large room, holding his daily *majlis*,[2] speaking with great energy and answering questions from his audience with clarity and humor. Humor is his hallmark; he even flirts with God, assured that His forgiveness is far greater than human sin, a supreme Sufi belief. The quality that distinguishes this great theologian of Khorasan[3] is his sense of humor and urbane literacy, one of the great clerics of eleventh-century Moslem Iran, he mixes poetry—his own or quotes from other poets—with his sermons, speaking with joy about the joy of life as a God-given inheritance of humankind. He is a devout Moslem, but, much to the chagrin of the authorities, he even has a few funny words to say about Islam.

A lowly man slips into the room and waits until the Sage stops talking, then approaches and leaves a leather bag, full of gold dinar coins. He is the manservant of a wealthy woman in town who has severe health problems, now alleviated; she has sent the Sage's portion of alms as a measure of thanksgiving and appreciation with the hope that Abu Sa'id will pray for herself and her family. The Sage can spend the money on himself or use it to feed the many who sit at his meals. All poor and indigent, all in need of a helping hand from God or man, and this man is considered an agent of God. Of course, he does not spend much money on himself but spreads all of his income among the dervishes and the Sufis, in *khaneghah*[4] or open-air feasts.

Abu Said stands and greets the lowly man and has him sit to his right, offers libations and food, and then sends him home with words of consolation to the servant and to his mistress. "Tell our sister her generosity is most welcome to the man who needs the gift!"

A dejected old man, a musician, is sitting on the slab of a stone covering a grave, playing his tambourine and praying. Tears run down his sallow cheeks; he cannot help but lament his condition, lacking home and shelter and dependent on the bakshish of passersby. He has remained in the graveyard for days as an appeal of last resort to God and His mercy. After all, hasn't the great Abu Sa'id admonished his followers to visit the graveyard daily for sober contemplation? Doesn't he visit the graveyard daily himself? All the musician asks for is enough money to build a shelter and a room for himself so he can play his music for the glory of Allah and the pleasure of His creatures: "O God, hear my prayers." He repeats his request, the final litany with increasing difficulty because he is losing control over his faculties and life.

Abu Sa'id calls his servant and whispers in his ear, "Take this bag of money to the musician in the graveyard. Do not shock him with a sudden move by untying the string of the purse, lest he faint and die. Just tell him, 'God heard your prayer and has answered it.' That is all, no other word. Then return immediately, no word of you or me!" The servant does his master's bidding and takes the money to the old musician. No one will know until Abu Sa'id's great-grandsons write their books about their famous ancestor and include this story, among other stories. The Sage never flaunted his generosity and acts of kindness, certainly.

Another time, the Sage is traveling, with a song on his lips, accompanied by an army of his followers when a small band of robbers waylays the troupe and demands Abu Sa'id's expensive horse. He dismounts and gives the reins to the thieves with a smile; his disciples object that they are many and the enemy but few and that they should fight and teach the robbers a lesson. Abu Sa'id prevails and prevents a fight. He says, "I have gifted the horse and will not take it back." The robbers leave but soon return, remorseful. They bring back the horse plus another good horse, its equal. Abu Sa'id again refuses to take his horse and the gift and sends the robbers away with his blessings.

These anecdotal stories point to several of Abu Sa'id's character traits. He was generous, of course, and he loved music as a divine gift. The old Sage of Mihaneh—as he is called by the name of his birthplace—never passed a musician who was playing an instrument without commencing to dance, even to the point that the other clerics more than frowned on his dancing in public. Enraged, they accused him of heresy and lewdness, which could have caused him great harm; the miracle was that it did not. He was so taken with dance and music—two Sufi spiritual rituals—that he ordered his followers to remain on their feet and continue to dance even when the muezzin called them from the minaret of the mosque to formal Islamic prayer. Dance, he said, and music are two gifts of God and sacramental: they are instruments of communication with God. Can there be a better way to talk to God than through music? If King David of the Old Testament was endowed by God to play his harp, Abu Sa'id reasoned, then God has given music for intense communication. After all, the muezzin who calls the devout to prayer sings his invitation with beautiful words from the holy book to bring to harmony those who will pray; the faithful listen to the cleric sing verses from the Koran. Ecstasy is the purest form of worship for the Sufi, and music induces euphoria to the point of dissolution in the Holy Spirit through the harmony of notes, rhythm, and movement.

A short time before his death, Abu Sa'id met with his disciples and offered suggestions for his own funeral. A disciple wrote down his instruction:

The Master said, "In my funeral
    Bring the drum—kus—and the players;
To my grave take me with steps of dance,
    Happy and with joy, drunk and clapping:
So they know the children of God
    Journey to Him with joy and laughter."
Another witness reported, "He said,
    Do not bring to my funeral, a man nor a woman,
        But a digger and a player of tar."[5]

Abu Sa'id was one of the early Sufis and an advocate of khaneghah, "the house," where the dervishes gathered. There, most of their theological thoughts were normalized and put into a system that would become a blueprint for the mystics of Persian and Arabic thought and, later, an influence on western mysticism. Hafez, if he was a Sufi, could not have said what he said without Abu Sa'id's pioneer work in building khaneghahs and practicing Sufi thoughts. One could think of khaneghah as a version of a monastery, a place that the dervishes gathered, argued, played music, danced, and ate. A home complete with family members, it was a fitting work for a man with the stature and vision of Abu Sa'id.

His generosity was not confined to material things; he was supremely generous of soul and mind, ever willing to forgive any slights to himself—or grave sins; he lived his life without being judgmental and accusing. The story goes that he was visiting the city of Tus[6] and asked for Seyyed Hamzeh, a man of eminence and wealth. Abu Sa'id was told he could not see him because Seyyed Hamzeh was indisposed, in the midst of a forty-day-and-night orgy and debauchery. He had ordered his men and women servants to remove their clothes and drink to intoxication and undertake licentious acts. The Sage replied, "Wonders! With his high position and spirit he could not commit any lesser sins!" and fell silent. The next day, when Seyyed Hamzeh was informed of the Sage's visit, he immediately sobered and rushed to the presence of Abu Sa'id. The Sage of Mihaneh greeted him warmly and sat him to his right, never mentioning a word of what he had heard. This is an amazing testament to the early education of Abu Sa'id, who, in his youth, lived in the desert under terrible conditions as a hermit and a recluse. His soul developed to the point that he never thought any sin unredeemable. To prove his point, he was fond of repeating the words of Mohammad, the Prophet of God, who said, "Any who does not accept the apology of a sinner—true or false—cannot drink from my wellspring."

The son of an intellectual apothecary—a scientist of his time—Abu Sa'id was exposed very early in life to enlightenment, Sufi enlightenment that subscribed to the idea that God is available for the asking without intermediaries and formalized rituals. As with the nineteenth-century western mystic–poets—such as William Wordsworth and Samuel Taylor Coleridge—the idea was to lose control of the body over self and to allow the spirit to dance and light the way. One way of unburdening the weight of matter is through dancing, slowly, then faster and faster until the body fatigues and collapses and the spirit lifts self to awareness. The present-day whirling dervishes in Turkey have their ancestry in this notion. Certainly Abu Sa'id subscribed to this idea. According to the earlier thinking of the Sage, the body was a burden of which to be divested. One way to do this was to go to the desert and live the life of a hermit by torturing the body into obedience. Certainly his early masters, such as Ghassab, were inclined to this kind of catharsis.

For two decades, Abu Sa'id continued the life of a mortifying fakir, living in caves, dependent on the generosity of passersby for subsistence. In the merciless sun, he often searched for weeds and thornbushes so as to extract a meager meal from their roots. Later, he repented such acts and would order his disciples to respect their bodies as God-given gifts, temples, loaned by the Almighty for a purposeful life. As a matter of fact, he openly suggested luxury, but for all, not just for himself, a matter that agitated two clerics so intensely that they wrote to Sultan Mahmud Ghaznavi, the ruler of the time, and accused Abu Sa'id of heresy, frivolity, and luxury. The letter they sent reads like a line from a satirical tract: Abu Sa'id and his friends eat roasted birds, cookies, and desserts and recite verses to each other instead of serious sermons and prayer. In other words, they are practicing paganism, not Islam. If the wise king had been so inclined, he could have Abu Sa'id killed, but it did not happen.

Abu Sa'id argued that self-torture is a selfish act because the purpose of such is the killing of "I"—"id" in Freudian terms, or "ego" as Jung would describe it—in order to squelch desires and passions, an impossible task. One becomes so absorbed in self-torture and addicted to it that it becomes an end in itself: Instead of negating passion, it strengthens desires and passions, feeding self-righteous hubris and arrogance.

Although he renounced mortification, Abu Sa'id had been exposed to it for such a long, extended time that he must have understood both its benefits and pains; nevertheless, he decried self-inflicted pain and counseled his followers to be on their guard and to disallow it from crippling their lives. However, since the world is filled with suffering, he considered pain a necessary component of living and sympathized with those under duress. Suffering in life must be accepted with courage and endurance.

At times a desert hermit, Abu Sa'id Abu Kheyr rose to the ranks of the Sheiks, though he uncharacteristically celebrated body and soul, contending that it is through an appreciation of the flesh that one can transcend and see the "other." Thus, for him art is essential for finding the thread of soul and the mystical "unknown." He writes:

> The world but a path, paradise a way station:
>> Both straws to discerning eyes.
> If a true lover, pass them by:
>> The Friend will show you His path.

Most of Abu Sa'id's poetry is in the quatrain form, later to be emulated and perfected by Omar Khayyám.[7] He wrote a number of *ghazals* and passion poems, but they are of lesser consequence. It is his quatrains (400 to 950 in number) that became the foundation on which Rumi and Hafez would build. Although he has rarely been translated into English, a few of the quatrains were included in A. J. Arberry's collections, and early in the twentieth century the *Journal of the Asiatic Society,* in Bengal, India, published a limited number of poorly translated English texts. The West is practically unaware of this poet; nevertheless, the time is ripe for him to be introduced to the English-speaking community. He will excite more than an academic interest in the reader because he is an artist first and theologian second and because his exquisite poetry is sheer delight to read, ready to be set to music and sung. I suspect that he will have the same kind of reception Rumi found a few years ago with the publication of Coleman Barks's translations.

Abu Sa'id wrote in the eleventh century; he was born in A.D. 967 and died around A.D. 1040 at the age of 83, making him in fact a tenth-century intellect. To put this in perspective, let me mention that William the Conqueror occupied England in 1066, and *Beowulf* was perhaps written and compiled just a century earlier. Chaucer would write four centuries in the future. The French language had only recently split from the Vulgate Latin, and the Old French *La Chanson de Roland* would be composed in the twelfth century. The Troubadour songs of Provence and the *Breton Lais* of Marie de France would not be composed for another two centuries. What is more, none of these western literary works are readable today unless one has training in Old English and Old French— Shakespeare and Dante are too modern to enter into our discussion—but Abu Sa'id is as available to modern readers as he was to his contemporaries.

This continuity in the intellectual and artistic energy of Iran is what distinguishes the Iranian culture from other traditions: one need not have special training in language or traditions to enjoy Hafez or Abu Sa'id fully. Abu Sa'id was himself immersed in the Islamic tradition of the time, and his early training was in theology and philosophy. Later, as a cleric of reputation, he incorporated his poetry into his sermons, thus marrying his art with his God, which resulted in a number of passion poems and mystical songs. His take on theology was unorthodox for the time because he preached tolerance and acceptance, and his quatrains especially speak of a God who is all merciful and all forgiving, even of those who do not follow the straight path of Islam. This perhaps raised eyebrows among the more dogmatic clerics. Professor Nafisi writes, "[He] established the kind of Sufism that is markedly different from the Sufism of Iraq ...Egypt and the west. For one, he considered the adherents of different religions equal and would not admit superiority to Islam."[8] Abu Sa'id pleads:

> Come, come again—whoever—come again:
>> If a pagan, a magus, an idolater, come again.
> Our threshold is not for despairing:
>> If a thousand times you break faith, come again.[9]

Of course, many of Abu Sa'id's quatrains are purely physical poems of love, and some purely metaphysical. But often, they are both: soul and body combined together and expressed in four-line poems, love of God and love of man coming together in hymns of extraordinary beauty, music, and content. It should be easy to see the doublethread of deep structure as one continues to read and study Abu Sa'id. But, then, there are those poems which are so complex that an easy judgment is impossible. Consider the following quatrain:

> You, who hasn't cancelled a word of this or that:
>> A second thought, remoter reason for the line.
> In the sentence of the universe, without error or mistake
> Take an *'yen* for body and only a *zát* for essence.

Here we have a play on letters and numbers: In English, it is an almost incomprehensible poem, a more poetic phrasing to express a mere enigma than a cogent poetic thought. Abu Sa'id uses Persian grammatical terms to construct his enigma. 'Yen and zát are names for two graphemes in the Persian/Arabic alphabet, but they both also have lexical meanings: nature, substance, intrinsic essence. In the first line he uses the word *khat*, meaning a line—or, even a scribbling—but in combination it also means "to cancel out, to disregard." And, in the first part of line three he uses *jomleh*, meaning a sentence, a phrase, but it also means "all." Through double entendre, the poet writes a perfectly delightful poem in Persian, but in English, what a problem! I have included this quatrain for explanatory reasons in the introduction, to show that no matter how a translator tries to be faithful to a text, there comes a time when he must simply gloss over the original and rewrite the intentions of the original text, thus abolishing it and creating something that is not really related to the original text! Or, in the following quatrain, in which the metaphysical and the sensual embrace with delightful effect:

In Hell, if I've a hold of your hair,
I'll shun the state of those in Heaven.
Without you, if I'm called to Heaven
Heaven will weigh heavily upon my heart.

However, a major problem still remains, a subject of much controversy and debate. Did Abu Sa'id write any of the poems attributed to him? Did he write even a single line of poetry, although the claim is that, as a child, he had memorized thirty thousand verses of poetry and could recite them on demand! Normally this would not have been a question to be discussed, although the authorship of the Shakespearian plays has been debated and much ink has been wasted in finding "the real playwright." Did Socrates really exist, or did Plato invent him?

The problem started very early in the canon of Abu Sa'id and in the works of his great-grandson, Mohammad ibn Monavvar, the author of *The Secrets of Oneness*, who wrote one of the two earliest critical biographies of Abu Sa'id just two generations after the death of the Sage. In the book Monavvar claims, "[I]t is said that the verses he uttered were his words; not so: he was not thus endowed and talented. Except for [the following] two lines, he wrote none."

My love, there is not a single thorn to my west
    That has no claim on me and my life!
Your favor and your beauty in my vision:
    I will give up a hundred-thousand lives!

The two sides have fought and written numerous tracts to prove their points and debunk their opponents; it has become a matter of honor to hold to personal convictions. Professor Nafisi, however, cites at least twelve sources and arguments why Abu Sa'id is the author of a number of these quatrains. His is the most authoritative source I have, although I have reviewed a number of scholarly sources on the matter. There is no doubt in my mind that a number of the poems are simply attributed to Abu Sa'id and the authorship is in doubt. I am equally convinced that at least 400 of the poems are his. All stylistic and historical evidences point to this fact, especially that some old sources name Abu Sa'id as the author of the poems. Then, the question is "Why do Mohammad

Monavvar[10] and Jamal-ad-Din Abu Ruh deny the authorship to their great-grandfather?"

Historically, the practitioners of arts have not been considered reputable and solid citizens of society. One can look at the attitude of English society toward actors at the time of Shakespeare; indeed, all the way to the early twentieth century they were considered to be licentious characters, scoundrels, and members of a class with low moral standing. The poets and even philosophers of early Islamic Iran were viewed in similar fashion. Although the kings and the nobles cherished the product of the poets' art, they rarely trusted the moral judgments of the poets. Abu Sa'id, an eminent cleric and theologian, would be a special target of suspicion if he "dabbled" in poetry and disgraced the name of his family. It is one thing to memorize the verses of other people and then to recite them as occasion arose, but it is another thing to be a "poet," a rather disreputable character of suspicious background. Monavvar, I suggest, was following the tradition of his time in trying to protect his great-grandfather's reputation. His is an act of expunging and revising the events. Fritz Meier correctly suggests that the "accuracy and truth of these two sources, because their authors have used every effort to glorify Abu Sa'id with exaggerated praises, are suspect. They have tried to portray him as a super-human being, above human foibles …at every turn disallowing any controversy about him."[11]

Personally, I do not think the matter is of great consequence. It is a fact that there are a number of beautifully constructed and well thought out poems that are in need of an author; it does not make much difference to me if Abu Sa'id wrote them, as it does not matter if a man called Shakespeare or

Bacon or Marlowe wrote a set of plays that are so exquisite and so beautiful—in any language. The fact is these poems *are*, and I am translating these poems regardless of their creators. Of course, it matters to know the "poet" who created them because a great deal of meaning can be elucidated from the biography of the poet. As is, it is the biography of Abu Sa'id that convinces many, including this translator, that the majority of the quatrains are from the pen of Abu Sa'id. I have chosen only those poems that have at least two corroborators of reputation, who consider the poems to belong to the Sage. Often I have three sources. I have included those that Nafisi and Saber-e Kermáni have included in their collections. Obviously, it is not within my province as a translator to ascertain the authenticity of my sources of translation. I must depend on the discretion of the established scholars and their vision to offer me guidelines. *I must defer to their judgment.* Honest people disagree with each other on the choice of the poems, but it is amazing how unanimous they are in their selections. If I found a disagreement between the two, I have often consulted a third and a fourth edition, all included in the bibliography.

Reza Ordoubadian, Ph.D.
March, 2009

Notes to Introduction

[1] The information provided in this introduction is based on two main sources that have traditionally been the wellspring for all other sources. The earliest biographies of Abu Sa'id were written by two of his great-grandsons, all the subsequent writings about him have primarily used these two volumes—*The Thoughts and Words of Abu Sa'id*, by Jamal al-Din Abu Ruh Lotfallah (1147 C.E.) and *The Secrets of Oneness in the Thoughts of Abu Sa'id* by Mohammad Ibn-Nur Ad-Din Monavvar (1178 and 1192 C.E.)—as their sources. These books were published for the first time by Valentin Zokovsky in St. Petersburg in 1899. I have not attempted to document every word I have written here for fear that footnotes would overwhelm the text, and this is the only acknowledgment I offer. There is no information in this introduction that cannot be verified in the text of these two sources, although the style of presentation is uniquely mine.

[2] Audience, meeting.

[3] Region that covered present-day northeastern Iran, western Afghanistan, and parts of Central Asia.

[4] A monastery, a gathering place for the Sufis.

[5] Mohammad Dámádi, *Abu Sa'id Nameh* (Tehran: University of Tehran Press, 1973), 60–61. The *tár* is a four-string musical instrument.

[6] A city in Greater Khorasan.

[7] Dámádi writes, "Ruba'is attributed to Abu Sa'id Abu Kheyr are among the first Persian Sufi poems [in Iran], and some have presented evidence that Hakim Omar Khayyám has followed Abu Sa'id in writing some of his ruba'is in Persian." See *Abu Sa'id Nameh*, 37.

[8] *Poetic Works of Abu Sa'id Abu Al-Kheyr*, 6th ed., edited and corrected by Sa'id Nafisi (Tehran: Sana'i Publishertttts, 1996), 6.

[9] Structurally, as in Anglo-Saxon poetry (e.g., *Beowulf*), all traditional Persian poetic lines are divided into two half-lines with a caesura in the middle. The term *quatrain* refers to four half-lines and two full lines. I suggest that most Persian poetry, as the traditional poetry of any other culture, was composed not so much to be recited as sung—even without accompanying musical instruments—either as chanting or as straight singing. The caesura technically allows a singer to catch his breath—certainly most singers were men—in the middle of the line and then continue to the second half. Persian music is commonly in minor key and uses quarter-tone notes and trilling. The rapid alternation of two tones, either a whole or a half tone apart in the voice, trilling requires a great amount of exhaling breath.

[10] Throughout his book, interestingly Monavvar goes on to attribute 96 quatrains to Abu Sa'id.

[11] Fritz Meier, *Abu Sa'id Abu Al-Kheyr: Myth or Truth*, translated by Mehr Afagh Boybordi (Tehran: Tehran University Press, 1976), 27.

The Poems of
Abu Sa'id
Abu'l Kheyr

۱

گفتم صنما لاله رخا دلدارا
در خواب نمای چهره باری یارا
گفتا که روی به خواب بی ما وانگه
خواهی که دگر به خواب بینی ما را

۲

وصل تو کجا و من مهجور کجا
دردانه کجا حوصله مور کجا
هر چند ز سوختن ندارم باکی
پروانه کجا و آتش طور کجا

1

I begged, "My idol, flower of my heart,
　　　　come to me in my dreams; show your face."
She answered, "Lover, you sleep without me; then
　　　　you want to dream of me in your sleep?"

2

What a chasm: Our union and my forlorn state of mind!
　　　　A single precious pearl and an ant's grasp!
Although unafraid of burning whole, yet I see
　　　　the disparity between a moth and the fire on Sinai![1]

٣

یا رب ز کرم دری برویم بگشا
راهی که درو نجات باشد بنما
مستغنیم از هر دو جهان کن به کرم
جز یاد تو هر چه هست بر از دل ما

٤

گر بر در دیر مینشانی ما را
گر در ره کعبه میدوانی ما را
اینها همگی لازمهٔ هستی ماست
خوش آنکه ز خویش وارهانی ما را

٥

مهمان تو خواهم آمدن جانانا
متواریک و ز حاسدان پنهانا
خالی کن این خانه، پس مهمان آ
با ما کس را به خانه در منشانا

3

O God, grace me with an open door:
        show me the path to salvation.
Your gift to me: freed of this world—and the other;
        your vision suffices: erase the rest from my heart.

4

If destined to knock at the door of the tavern,
        if fated to run the path around the Kaaba,[2]
these, preconditions of our existential self—
        blessed the day You rescue us from our *self*!

5

Lover, I, your guest, will steal to your house,
        secretly, hidden from the jealous eyes.
Empty your house for the guest to come—
        do not allow anyone but us in that house.

۶

کارم همه ناله و خروشست امشب
نی‌صبر پدیدست و نه هو شست امشب
دوشم خوش بود ساعتی پنداری
کفارهٔ خوشدلی دوشست امشب

۷

آنروز که آتش محبت افروخت
عاشق روش سوز ز معشوق آموخت
از جانب دوست سرزد این سوز و گداز
تا در نگرفت شمع پروانه نسوخت

۸

ایدل چو فراقش رگ جان بگشودت
منمای بکس خرقهٔ خون آلودت
می‌نال چنانکه نشنوند آوازت
می‌سوز چنانکه برنیاید دودت

6

I'm all crying and groans tonight;
        no patience bides, no reason rules tonight!
Yesternight in a dream-wink I imagined happiness:
        now, the time to atone my happiness tonight.

7

The day He blazed the fire of love,
        the lover learned the art of burning from his sweetheart.
This anguish, this fire came from the Friend—[3]
        until the candle flames, the moth[4] does not burn.

8

When the lover's absence bleeds your heart,
        do not show the bloodied garment to the crowd:
You groan, not to be heard—
        you burn, refusing to smolder.

تا چند کشم غصهٔ هر ناکس را
وز خِسَّت خود خاک شوم هر کس را
کارم به دعا چو برنمی‌آید راست
دادم سه طلاق این فلک اطلس را

یا رب مکن از لطف پریشان ما را
هر چند که هست جرم و عصیان ما را
ذات تو غنی بوده و ما محتاجیم
محتاج بغیر خود مگردان ما را

پرسیدم ازو واسطهٔ هجران را
گفتا سببی هست بگویم آن را
من چشم توام اگر نبینی چه عجب
من جان توام کسی نبیند جان را

9

How long will I suffer the burden of mean crowds?
By meanness, I'm like dirt spread at their feet.
Since my affairs will not right with prayers,
I'll thrice divorce[5] this silken dome.

10

O God, withhold not your grace from us:
ever sinful and rebellious we are.
Your nature, free of wants; ours, full of needs:
but, You—do not make us need anyone.

11

I asked, "Why this separation?"
The answer came, "There's a reason—listen!"
"I'm your eyes; no wonder—you see";
"I'm your soul—no one sees a soul."

۱۲

بازآ بازآ هر آنچه هستی بازآ
گر کافر و گبر و بت‌پرستی بازآ
این درگه ما درگه نومیدی نیست
صد بار اگر توبه شکستی بازآ

۱۳

مجنون تو کوه را ز صحرا نشناخت
دیوانهٔ عشق تو سر از پا نشناخت
هر کس بتو ره یافت ز خود گم گردید
آنکس که ترا شناخت خود را نشناخت

۱۴

در مدرسه گر چه دانش اندوز شوی
وز گرمی بحث مجلس افروز شوی
در مکتب عشق با همه دانایی
سر گشته چو طفلان نوآموز شوی

12

Come, come again—whoever—come again:
      if a pagan, a magus, an idolater, come again.
Our threshold is not for despairing:
      if a thousand times you break faith, come again.

13

Your crazed lover cannot tell a mountain from the desert:
      nor his head from his toe!
Anyone who finds You loses his self;
      anyone who knows You forgets himself.

14

In the schoolhouse you become a learner:
      from the warmth of discussions you glow.
In the school of love, with all your learning
      you become a wandering schoolboy.

دنیا راهی بهشت منزلگاهی

این هر دو به نزد اهل معنی کاهی

گر عاشق صادقی زهر دو بگذر

تا دوست ترا به خود نماید راهی

آن عشق که هست جزء لاینفک ما

حاشا که شود به عقل ما مدرک ما

خوش آنکه ز نور او دمد صبح یقین

ما را برهاند ز ظلام شک ما

در کعبه اگر دل سوی غیرست ترا

طاعت همه فسق و کعبه دیرست ترا

ور دل به خدا و ساکن میکده‌ای

می نوش که عاقبت بخیرست ترا

15

The world but a path, paradise a way station:
>   both straws to discerning eyes.
If a true lover, pass them by:
>   the Friend will show you His path.

16

Love, that essential fountain of our soul:
>   may it not become our witness only through our head.
Happy he from whom the dawn of conviction shines
>   to rescue us from the darkness of our doubts.

17

You're in the Kaaba, your heart wandering:
>   worshipping is for naught—Kaaba is disallowed!
Heart with God, you reside in the tavern:
>   drink your wine—you'll end up right.

۱۸

از بار گنه شد تن مسکینم پست
یا رب چه شود اگر مرا گیری دست
گر در عملم آنچه ترا شاید نیست
اندر کرمت آنچه مرا باید هست

۱۹

شیرین دهنی که از لبش جان میریخت
کفرش ز سر زلف پریشان میریخت
گر شیخ به کفر زلف او ره میبرد
خاک ره او بر سر ایمان میریخت

۲۰

سوفسطایی که از خرد بیخبرست
گوید عالم خیالی اندر گذرست
آری عالم همه خیالیست ولی
پیوسته حقیقتی درو جلوه گرست

18

I'm doubled by the burden of sins;
      O God, will you hold my hand?
If in my works what you wish is not seen,
      in your grace whatever I need is there!

19

Sweet lover scattering life from her lips,
      blasphemy falling from her tussled tresses.
If the sheik follows the blasphemy of her path,
      the dust of her path on the head of Faith he scatters.

20

A Sophist, innocent of wisdom,
      declares the world a passing fancy.
Granted! The world is nothing but a fiction, yet
      It reveals truths abundantly.

اسرار ملک بین که بغول افتادست
وان سکهٔ زر بین که بپول افتادست
وان دست برافشاندن مردان زد و کون
اکنون بترانهٔ کچول افتادست

ناکامیم ای دوست ز خودکامی تست
وین سوختگیهای من از خامی تست
مگذار که در عشق تو رسوا گردم
رسوایی من باعث بدنامی تست

در درد شکی نیست که درمانی هست
با عشق یقینست که جانانی هست
احوال جهان چو دم به دم میگردد
شک نیست درین حال که گردانی هست

21

Secrets of angels fall into the hands of the devil!
      And, that piece of Gold changes into a coin!
The dance of men in this world—and the other
      has now turned to a poisonous song.[6]

22

My demise, O friend, is from your conceit,
      my burning wound from your slight.
In your love, do not me disgrace:
      my shame, the source of your disgrace!

23

For every pain certainly a cure,
      for every love surely a lover.
The ever-changing affairs of life:
      no doubt a Mover for that, too.

۲۴

نقاش رخت ز طعنها آسودست
کز هر چه تمامتر بود بنمودست
رخسار و لبت چنانکه باید بودست
گویی که کسی برزو فرمودست

۲۵

در عالم اگر فلک اگر ماه و خورست
از بادهٔ مستی تو پیمانه خورست
فارغ زجهانی و جهان غیر تو نیست
بیرون زمکانی و مکان از تو پرست

۲۶

یا رب سبب حیات حیوان بفرست
وز خون کرم نعمت الوان بفرست
از بهر لب تشنهٔ طفلان نبات
از سینهٔ ابر شیر باران بفرست

24

Free of blame is the painter of your face:
    revealer of the wholeness of your soul.
Your visage, your lips, both as they should be,
    as if an inner wish has ordained that face.

25

If creation is this dome, this sun and this moon,
    then, from the wine of your drinking this cup is full.
Freed of this world, the world is nothing but You:
    beyond any space, of You the space is full!

26

O God, the elixir of life of anima—You send us;
    from the table of Your grace, a rainbow of gifts—send us.
For the thirsty lips of the children of the plants,
    from the breast of the clouds, a milk of rain—send us.

ای خالق خلق رهنمایی بفرست
بر بندهٔ بی‌نوا نوایی بفرست
کار من بیچاره گره در گرهست
رحمی بکن و گره گشایی بفرست

راه تو بهر روش که پویند خوشست
وصل تو بهر جهت که جویند خوشست
روی تو بهر دیده که بیند نکوست
نام تو بهر زبان که گویند خوشست

نردیست جهان که بردنش باختنست
نرادی او بنقش کم ساختنست
دنیا بمثل چو کعبتین نردست
برداشتنش برای انداختنست

27

O Author of man—send us a guide;
      to the stale life of your creatures—send a melody![7]
Poor me! My affairs all entangled: knot upon knot;
      show mercy and untie my knots!

28

Reaching you by any path is welcome;
      union with you in any land is welcome.
Your face through any eyes is pleasant;
      your name uttered in any tongue is welcome.[8]

29

Life but a game of backgammon,[9] winning is losing;
      the skill is in reducing.
The world like a pair of dice:
      picking them is for throwing.

آواز در آمد بنگر یار منست
من خود دانم کرا غم کار منست
سیصد گل سرخ بر رخ یار منست
خیزم بچنم که گل چدن کار منست

پرسید ز من کسیکه معشوق تو کیست
گفتم که فلان کسست مقصود تو چیست
بنشست و به‌های‌های بر من بگریست
کز دست چنان کسی تو چون خواهی زیست

جسمم همه اشک گشت و چشمم بگریست
در عشق تو بی جسم همی باید زیست
از من اثری نماند این عشق ز چیست
چون من همه معشوق شدم عاشق کیست

The voice came, "Look! It's my love;
      I know it: her affairs the cause of my woes."
"A hundred roses adorn her face;
      I'll rise for a bud: picking flowers is my role!"

31

He asked me, "Who's your lover?"
      I said, "Such and such; and your purpose?"
He sat, tears running from his eyes—and said:
      "In the hands of such lover—how can you persist?"

32

My body turns to tears, but my eyes cry;
      for your love my flesh I give.
No flesh left now; whence this love comes?
      Since I am the beloved, who is my lover, then?

دیروز که چشم تو بمن در نگریست
خلقی بهزار دیده بر من بگریست
هر روز هزار بار در عشق تو ام
میباید مرد و باز میباید زیست

گر کار تو نیکست به تدبیر تو نیست
ور نیز بدست هم ز تقصیر تو نیست
تسلیم و رضا پیشه کن و شاد بزی
چون نیک و بد جهان به تقدیر تو نیست

در کشور عشق جای آسایش نیست
آنجا همه کاهشست افزایش نیست
بی درد و الم توقع درمان نیست
بی جرم و گنه امید بخشایش نیست

33

Yesterday, when your eyes stole a glance at me:
  with a thousand eyes men wept for me.
A thousand times a day I fall for you:
  one must die—and again, one must live!

34

If successful, it's not your planning;
  failing is not your fault.
Accept your lot—be happy:
  Are you in command of your lot?

35

No respite in the land of Love:
  there—all is subtraction, no rise;
No pain and suffering, no hope of healing,
  no sin or guilt, no hope of redeeming.

روزم به غم جهان فرسوده گذشت
شب در هوس بوده و نابوده گذشت
عمری که ازو دمی جهانی ارزد
القصه به فکرهای بیهوده گذشت

آنرا که قضا ز خیل عشاق نوشت
آزاد ز مسجدست و فارغ ز کنشت
دیوانهٔ عشق را چه هجران چه وصال
از خویش گذشته را چه دوزخ چه بهشت

ای با رخت انوار مه و خور همه هیچ
با لعل تو سلسبیل و کوثر همه هیچ
بودم همه بین، چو تیزبین شد چشمم
دیدم که همه تویی و دیگر همه هیچ

36

My days choked in the woes of this weary world,
     my night I wasted grieving my losses and my gains:
A breath of life is worth the sum of all this world—
     yet, I spent my life in nonconsequential thoughts.

37

Those fated to the ranks of the lovers,
     free are they from Mosque and Synagogue.
For the mad lover it matters not parted or united.
     If delivered of self, what if in heaven or in hell!

38

Your face shames the light of the moon and sun;
     your lips sweeter than the nectar in paradise.
My roaming eyes searched for your face, finding,
     I understood: you are all, and all is for naught![10]

گر عشق دل مرا خریدار افتد
کاری بکنم که پرده از کار افتد
سجادهٔ پرهیز چنان افشانم
کز هر تاری هزار زنار افتد

گویند که محتسب گمانی ببرد
وین پردهٔ تو پیش جهانی بدرد
گویم که ازین شراب اگر محتسبست
دریابد قطره‌ای به جانی بخرد

از چهرهٔ عاشقانه‌ام زر بارد
وز چشم ترم همیشه آذر بارد
در آتش عشق تو چنان بنشینم
کز ابر محبتم سمندر بارد

39

If love ever purchases my heart,
      I will do all to unveil that secret.
I'll tear the prayer rug of caution that
      from every fiber a thousand zonárs[11] rise.

40

They say the censor[12] is suspicious:
      he'll rend your curtain of secrets.
I say, if from this wine the censor
      tastes a drop, he'll buy it with his soul!

41

From my lovesick face yellow gold rains,
      from my teary eyes fire always rains.
I'll sit in the fire of your love
      from the clouds of my love, salamander[13] rains.

۴۲

اندر همه دشت خاوران سنگی نیست
کش با من و روزگار من جنگی نیست
با لطف و نوازش وصال تو مرا
دردادن صد هزار جان ننگی نیست

۴۳

دل گر چه درین بادیه بسیار شتافت
یک موی ندانست و بسی موی شکافت
گرچه ز دلم هزار خورشید بتافت
آخر به کمال ذره‌ای راه نیافت

۴۴

با علم اگر عمل برابر گردد
کام دو جهان ترا میسر گردد
مغرور مشو به خود که خواندی ورقی
زان روز حذر کن که ورق بر گردد

42

Not a single stone in all the deserts of the East
　　　exists that has no quarrel with me and my times.
But if favored by your love and caresses,
　　　I'll offer my life a thousand times.

43

My heart rushed—traversed this vast desert.
　　　No! I did not learn a whit, but lost my hair.
From my heart a thousand suns glowed, yet
　　　the loss is mine: Did I learn a whit?

44

Wisdom and deed, if they combine,
　　　this and the other world are possible.
Hubris filled for having read a page,
　　　beware of the day when the page is turned.

۴۵

گل از تو چراغ حسن در گلشن برد
وز روی تو آیینه دل روشن برد
هر خانه که شمع رخت افروخت درو
خورشید چو ذره نور از روزن برد

۴۶

گر پنهان کرد عیب و گر پیدا کرد
منت دارم ازو که بس برجا کرد
تاج سر من خاک سر پای کسیست
کو چشم مرا به عیب من بینا کرد

۴۷

گفتار دراز مختصر باید کرد
وز یار بدآموز حذر باید کرد
در راه نگار کشته باید گشتن
و آنگاه نگار را خبر باید کرد

45

Rose takes beauty to the garden from your face;
        from your eyes[14] the mirror of my heart ignites.
A home lit by the candle of your face
        hosts a sliver of sun flowing from a crystal pane.

46

If he hid it or he divulged my flaws, I'm
        indebted to his grace for the truth of his act.
The crown of my head, dirt at his feet
        who opens my eyes to see my fault.

47

Cut a long story short,
        avoid ignorant mates.
Be slain on the way to your lover,
        then inform her of your case!

خرم دل آنکه از ستم آه نکرد
کس را ز درون خویش آگاه نکرد
چون شمع ز سوز دل سراپا بگداخت
وز دامن شعله دست کوتاه نکرد

آن دشمن دوست بود دیدی که چه کرد
یا اینکه بغور او رسیدی که چه کرد
میگفت همان کنم که خواهد دل تو
دیدی که چه میگفت و شنیدی که چه کرد

من صرفه برم که بر صفم اعدا زد
مشتی خاک لطمه بر دریا زد
ما تیغ برهنه‌ایم در دست قضا
شد کشته هر آنکه خویش را بر ما زد

Happy he who never complains of injustice,
      does not divulge the secret of his heart.
A candle, head to toe consuming,
      does not cringe from the heat of the flame!

49

That foe, the friend, did you see what he did?
      Or, reach his depths and see what he did?
He said, "I promise: Your wish is my desire."
      Did you see what he said and hear what he did?[15]

50

If enemy plunge at my ranks—I profit:
      a handful of dust the greater sea blemishes!
We're a drawn sword in the hand of Fate:
      he died who plunged himself at our self!

عارف بچنین روز کناری گیرد
یا دامن کوه و لاله‌زاری گیرد
از گوشهٔ میخانه پناهی طلبد
تا عالم شوریده قراری گیرد

انواع خطا گر چه خدا می‌بخشد
هر اسم عطیه‌ای جدا می‌بخشد
در هر آنی حقیقت عالم را
یک اسم فنا یکی بقا می‌بخشد

دلخسته و سینه چاک می‌باید شد
وز هستی خویش پاک می‌باید شد
آن به که به خود پاک شویم اول کار
چون آخر کار خاک می‌باید شد

51

Of a day the Gnostic might retire
      or seek solace from the garden and hills.
Oh, if he seek shelter at the tavern,
      the whole frenzied world settles!

52

Although our Lord forgives our sins,
      each name a different gift He gives.
Any moment, the truth of the universe:
      one name mortality and the other eternity he gives.

53

Heart sore, afflicted I must live;
      my being I must rinse.
Better at the start of our game:
      at the end to dust we must turn.

زان پیش که طاق چرخ اعلا زده‌اند
وین بارگه سپهر مینا زده‌اند
ما در عدم آباد ازل خوش خفته
بی ما رقم عشق تو بر ما زده‌اند

آنروز که نقش کوه و هامون بستند
ترکیب سهی قدان موزون بستند
پا بسته به زنجیر جنون من بودم
مردم سخنی به پای مجنون بستند

هوشم نه موافقان و خویشان بردند
این کج کلهان مو پریشان بردند
گویند چرا تو دل بدیشان دادی
والله که من ندادم ایشان بردند

54

Before the Arch of the Grand Wheel was fixed,
    before the Court at the azured Heavens was set—
We, wonderfully sleeping in the city of our pre-existence—
    without us, Your love was written for us to plan.

55

That day! When He was fashioning mountains and lands,
    when he designed the elegant form of man:
I was chained to my love-madness,
    but the credit went to the Majnun man.[16]

56

My mind, I lost it not to my friend or my kin;
    it was stolen by those devious beauties with flowing hair.
They blame: why did you give your heart to such?
    God knows; I did not give—they stole it!

۵۷

در دیر شدم ماحضری آوردند
یعنی ز شراب ساغری آوردند
کیفیت او ز خود بیخود کرد
بردند مرا و دیگری آوردند

۵۸

یارم همه نیش بر سر نیش زند
گویم که مزن ستیزه را بیش زند
چون در دل من مقام دارد شب و روز
میترسم از آنکه نیش بر خویش زند

۵۹

آن کس که به کوه ظلم خرگاه زند
خود را به دم آه سحرگاه زند
ای راهزن از دور مکافات بترس
راهی که زنی ترا همان راه زند

I went to my tavern;[17] they brought a simple meal:
      a jug of wine it was they served.
Its nature made a difference in me:
      they took me away, another me they left!

58

Her biting tongue, my love stings over sting;
      I say, "stop!" She only increases her bites.
In my heart she resides day and night:
      I fear she might sting herself!

59

Pitch a tent on the mountain of oppressions, and
      you will hear the sad sighs of the Zephyr.
Oh, you robber, fear your karma:
      the highway you rob today will rob you tomorrow.

۶۰

در مدرسه اسباب عمل می‌بخشند
در میکده لذت ازل می‌بخشند
آنجا که بنای خانهٔ رندانست
سرمایهٔ ایمان به سبل می‌بخشند

۶۱

نقاش اگر ز موی پرگار کند
نقش دهن تنگ تو دشوار کند
آن تنگی و نازکی که دارد دهنت
ترسم که نفس لب تو افگار کند

۶۲

در چنگ غم تو دل سرودی نکند
پیش تو فغان و ناله سودی نکند
نالیم به ناله‌ای که آگه نشوی
سوزیم به آتشی که دودی نکند

60

At school the gift is practical matters;
     at the tavern, eternal pleasure.
At the house of rendán[18]
     "The hell with the wages of faith!"

61

The painter, if he fashions his brush[19] from a single hair
     hardly will he succeed in painting your narrow lips.
The narrow lips, your delicate mouth,
     I fear he'll wound the breath flowing from your mouth!

62

For your sorrowing, my heart cannot sing;[20]
     for you, my lamenting and sighs are futile.
Silently, I will grieve: you will hear not my voice.
     I will burn in my passion: no smoke you will see.

خواهی که خدا کار نکو با تو کند
ارواح ملایک همه رو با تو کند
یا هر چه رضای او در آنست بکن
یا راضی شو هر آنچه او با تو کند

عاشق که تواضع ننماید چه کند
شبها که به کوی تو نیاید چه کند
گر بوسه دهد زلف ترا رنجه مشو
دیوانه که زنجیر نخاید چه کند

گر عدل کنی بر جهانت خوانند
ور ظلم کنی سگ عوانت خوانند
چشم خردت باز کن و نیک ببین
تا زین دو کدام به که آنت خوانند

63

You who yearn for the Grace of God—
      the angels' gaze showering your soul?
Do whatever is His pleasure;
      otherwise, accept whatever is His pleasure.

64

The lover, what can he do but to obey?
      What can he do if not wander your alley?
Do not be alarmed if he air-kisses your hair.
      What can a mad lover do, if not chew his chains?

65

Be just and you're judged a pious man,
      Cruel, a bloody cur!
Open your inner eyes—see
      which name is yours!

گه زاهد تسبیح به دستم خوانند
گه رند و خراباتی و مستم خوانند
ای وای به روزگار مستوری من
گر زانکه مرا چنانکه هستم خوانند

شب خیز که عاشقان به شب راز کنند
گرد در و بام دوست پرواز کنند
هر جا که دری بود به شب بربندند
الا در عاشقان که شب باز کنند

مردان رهش میل به هستی نکنند
خودبینی و خویشتن پرستی نکنند
آنجا که مجردان حق می نوشند
خم خانه تهی کنند و مستی نکنند

66

For a time, they called me a rosary-bearing pious ascetic,
    for a time, a rend,[21] a drunk of the taverns;
Oh, the pain of this concealment of the truth
    if one day they call me what I really am!

67

Lovers whisper secrets at night—wake up sleepyhead—
    round the lover's door and rooftop they fly.
Wherever a door, it is bolted at night
    except the door to the lover's heart!

68

The enlightened do not give their heart to the world,
    .do not indulge in self-conceit nor in selfish thought.
Where the elect drink their wine
    the vat is empty, but they are not drunk![22]

دشمن چو به ما درنگرد بد بیند
عیبی که بر ماست یکی صد بیند
ما آینه‌ایم، هر که در ما نگرد
هر نیک و بدی که بیند از خود بیند

در عشق تو گاه بت پرستم گویند
گه رند و خراباتی و مستم گویند
اینها همه از بهر شکستم گویند
من شاد به اینکه هر چه هستم گویند

رفتم به کلیسیای ترسا و یهود
دیدم همه با یاد تو در گفت و شنود
با یاد وصال تو به بتخانه شدم
تسبیح بتان زمزمه ذکر تو بود

69

Our antagonist eyes us: sees—we're all flawed!
    Each defect he sees a hundredfold.
Yet! A mirror we are; any who gazes at us,
    any good he sees or bad, it's his face—on us.[23]

70

For your love, I'm called an idolater,
    often, a rend, a drunk of the tavern.
All this just to break my soul,
    but happy I to be called the man—I am!

71

I sauntered to a church and then a synagogue:
    Lo! Everyone with Your name—conversant!
In hope of our union, I took my path to the idol-house:
    chaplet in hand, the idols were murmuring Your name.

اول رخ خود به ما نبایست نمود
تا آتش ما جای دگر گردد دود
اکنون که نمودی و ربودی دل ما
ناچار ترا دلبر ما باید بود

آنروز که بنده آوریدی به وجود
میدانستی که بنده چون خواهد بود
یا رب تو گناه بنده بر بنده مگیر
کین بنده همین کند که تقدیر تو بود

ز اول ره عشق تو مرا سهل نمود
پنداشت رسد به منزل وصل تو زود
گامی دو سه رفت و راه را دریا دید
چون پای درون نهاد موجش بربود

Your Face! You should never have shown It:
      elsewhere our fire would have smoldered!
Yet, You have—and stolen our heart; now
      no escaping: You certainly are our Sweetheart.[24]

73

The day You fashioned your man,
      You knew the way of his ways!
Judge not, O God, his failings:
      he does as You've ordained him!

74

The way to your love seemed so simple,
      I thought, easy to reach consummation.
Two steps, and the path turned into an ocean:
      the water touched my foot—the waves stole it!

گر ملک تو شام و گر یمن خواهد بود
وز سر حد چین تا به ختن خواهد بود
روزی که ازین سرا کنی عزم سفر
همراه تو هفت گز کفن خواهد بود

زان ناله که در بستر غم دوشم بود
غمهای جهان جمله فراموشم بود
یاران همه درد من شنیدند ولی
یاری که درو کرد اثر گوشم بود

آن وقت که این انجم و افلاک نبود
وین آب و هوا و آتش و خاک نبود
اسرار یگانگی سبق می‌گفتم
وین قالب و این نوا و ادارک نبود

If your kingdom stretches from Damascus to Yaman:
     if from the borders of China to Khotan:[25]
The day you set to travel from this land,
     your company will be seven gaz[26] of kaftan.[27]

76

Groaning in the bed of my woes,
     I forgot all other cares of life.
My friends all heard of my pain:
     my ears, the only friend who responded!

77

There was a time: stars and heavens did not exist,
     no air or water, nor fire or earth.
I could've told of the Unity of our Source,
     but there was no form, no light, nor music of the spheres.

جایی که تو باشی اثر غم نبود
آنجا که نباشی دل خرم نبود
آن را که ز فرقت تو یک دم نبود
شادیش زمین و آسمان کم نبود

نه کس که زجور دهر افسرده نبود
نی گل که درین زمانه پژمرده نبود
آنرا که بیامدست زیبا آمد
دانی که بیامده چو آورده نبود

هر چند که جان عارف آگاه بود
کی در حرم قدس تواش راه بود
دست همه اهل کشف و ارباب شهود
از دامن ادراک تو کوتاه بود

78

A profanation to grieve when you are present,
        a cruelty of the heart when you are absent.
Yet, in my life your constant presence
        surpasses the happiness on this earth and in heaven.

79

Who is untouched by the ravage of time?
        What flower remains unwithered in time?
Beautifully welcome those who come,
        but they're unlike those invited to come.[28]

80

The soul of the Gnostic knows—
        he is privy to your Holy thoughts.
Yet the reach of such initiated man
        is far short of your discernment and lore.

هر کو ز در عمر درآید برود
چیزیش بجز غم نگشاید برود
از سر سخن کسی نشانی ندهد
ژاژی دو سه هر کسی بخاید برود

عاشق که غم جان خرابش نرود
تا جان بود از جان تب و تابش نرود
خاصیت سیماب بود عاشق را
تا کشته نگردد اضطرابش نرود

در دل چو کجیست روی بر خاک چه سود
چون زهر به دل رسید تریاک چه سود
تو ظاهر خود به جامه آراسته‌ای
دلهای پلید و جامهٔ پاک چه سود

The gates of life admit you—then out you go:
        nothing avails you here, but woe!
No one gives any sign of the mystery of Word:
        a few idly talk, each to each—then you go![29]

82

A lover unravished by the woes of life—
        living, will not yield his glow and his fever.
The lover's nature is the quicksilver's:
        unless slain,[30] will not cease to tremble.

83

The heart is crooked! What use a humble pretense?
        The poison has reached the heart! What use the cure?
Adorned with garments fine:
        What use clean garments, heart defiled?

روزی که چراغ عمر خاموش شود
در بستر مرگ عقل مدهوش شود
با بی دردان مکن خدایا حشرم
ترسم که محبتم فراموش شود

گر دشمن مردان همگی حرق شود
هم برق صفت به خویشتن برق شود
گر سگ به مثل درون دریا برود
دریا نشود پلید و سگ غرق شود

هرگز دلم از یاد تو غافل نشود
گر جان بشود مهر تو از دل نشود
افتاده ز روی تو در آیینهٔ دل
عکسی که به هیچ وجه زایل نشود

84

The day the lamp of life is doused,
       in death's throes human mind drowns.
O God do not put me among the unsuffered:
       I fear my affection and love will suffer!

85

If all the enemies of men burn,
       A scintillating nature becomes its own glow.
If a dog walks into the ocean:
       the water never spoils; the dog drowns![31]

86

Neglect you! Never in my life:
       I live, so your love remains in my heart.
Your face in the mirror of my heart reflected,
       a picture never to be faded!

۸۷

آن رشته که بر لعل لبت سوده شود
وز نوش دهانت اشک آلوده شود
خواهم که بدین سینهٔ چاکم دوزی
شاید که زغمهای تو آسوده شود

۸۸

گفتی که شب آیم ارچه بیگاه شود
شاید که زبان خلق کوتاه شود
بر خفته کجا نهان توانی کردن
کز بوی خوش تو مرده آگاه شود

۸۹

ار کشتن من دو چشم مست خواهد
شک نیست که طبع بت پرستت خواهد
ترسنده از آنم که اگر بر دستت
من کشته شوم که عذر دستت خواهد

That woven piece, kiss-touching your ruby lips,
  teary from the taste of the nectar of your mouth:
Stitch it on my chest, rent and wounded;
  mayhap I'll be freed from your woes.

You said, "Come late—at night—though inconvenient;
  perhaps the babble of the neighbors will cease."
I said, "How can you hide from those—asleep;
  your sweet scent arouses those—dead!"

That look in your besotted eyes desires my death—
  no doubt—your pagan nature desires my death.
I fear if killed by your hands
  you'll have no one to be your alibi!

آورد صبا گلی ز گلزار امید
یا روح قدس شهپری افگند سفید
یا کرد صبا شق ورقی از خورشید
یا نامهٔ یارست که آورد نوید

گوشم چو حدیث درد چشم تو شنید
فی‌الحال دلم خون شد و از دیده چکید
چشم تو نکو شود به من چون نگری
تا کور شود هر آنکه نتواند دید

هر چند که دیده روی خوب تو ندید
یک گل ز گلستان وصال تو نچید
اما دل سودا زده در مدت عمر
جز وصف جمال تو نه گفت و نه شنید

90

A rose from the garden of hopes the breeze delivered;
      or, was it a white feather the Holy Spirit sent?
Perhaps, the Zephyr dropped a slice of the shining sun!
      Or, it's the letter of the lover with a hopeful note.

91

My ears hear the pain in your eyes:
      anon my heart bleeds from my eyes.
Your eyes will heal: look upon me.
      Sightless he—who cannot bear to see.

92

Though my eyes did not see your better side,
      from the garden of union did not pick a rose:
Yet, during life my melancholic heart,
      but in praise of your face—did utter not a single word.

۹۳

در باغ روم کوی توام یاد آید
بر گل نگرم روی توام یاد آید
در سایهٔ سرو اگر دمی بنشینم
سرو قد دلجوی توام یاد آید

۹۴

در دوزخم ار زلف تو در چنگ آید
از حال بهشتیان مرا ننگ آید
ور بی تو به صحرای بهشتم خوانند
صحرای بهشت بر دلم تنگ آید

۹۵

ای خواجه ز فکر گور غم میباید
اندر دل و دیده سوز و نم میباید
صد وقت برای کار دنیا داری
یک وقت به فکر گور هم میباید

93

I go to the garden, your face haunts me;
     I look at a flower, your face haunts me.
I rest for a bit under a juniper,[32]
     your beauteous body haunts me!

94

In hell, if I've a hold of your hair,
     I'll shun the state of those in heaven.
Without you, if I'm called to heaven,
     heaven will weigh heavily upon my heart.

95

O Master,[33] you must think of the grave:
     heart in pain, eyes filled with tears.
A hundred times for the affairs of this world:
     just once think of the grave!

۹۶

چشمی به سحاب همنشین می‌باید
خاطر به نشاط خشمگین می‌باید
سر بر سر دار و سینه بر سینهٔ تیغ
آسایش عاشقان چنین می‌باید

۹۷

ای عشق به درد تو سری می‌باید
صید تو ز من قوی‌تری می‌باید
من مرغ به یک شعله کبابم بگذار
کین آتش را سمندری می‌باید

۹۸

آسان گل باغ مدعا نتوان چید
بی سرزنش خار جفا نتوان چید
بشکفته گل مراد بر شاخ امید
تا سر ننهی به زیر پا نتوان چید

An eye on the far clouds[34] of the friend—keeping,
      heart angry with gladness—feeling.
Neck to the noose, breast to the point of sword:
      such is the comfort of the lovers—reeling!

97

My love! Your demands are much:
      pursuing you requires stronger hunter.
I'm a bird, on a single tongue of flame roasting:
      the fire you set requires salamander.[35]

98

Not easy to pick roses in the garden of affectations:
      without the blame of the thorn unkindness cannot be pared.
The flower of wishes blossoms on the tree of hopes:
      unless the head is put under the feet, you cannot reach it!

جانم به لب از لعل خموش تو رسید
از لعل خموش باده نوش تو رسید
گوش تو شنیده‌ام که دردی دارد
درد دل من مگر به گوش تو رسید

گلزار وفا ز خار من می‌روید
اخلاص ز رهگذار من می‌روید
در فکر تو دوش سر به زانو بودم
امروز گل از کنار من می‌روید

تا چند حدیث قامت و زلف نگار
تا کی باشی تو طالب بوس و کنار
گر زانکه نه‌ای دروغزن عاشق‌وار
در عشق چو او هزار چون او بگذار

99

My patience wears, your ruby lips silent:
　　　　your wine-sipping ruby lips silent.
Your ears, I hear, suffer from some pain:
　　　　did the pain of my heart reach your ears?

100

The garden of fidelity flourishes from my thorn;
　　　　sincerity flowers on the path of my way.[36]
Yesternight, head bent on knees, I was of your thought:
　　　　today, a flower garden grows by my side.

101

How long the fable of the lover's hair and her face?
　　　　How long desiring her kisses and her bed?
If no lover's lies live on your tongue—
　　　　in such a love pass by a thousand like her.

چشمم که نداشت تاب نظارهٔ یار
شد اشک فشان به پیش آن سیم عذار
در سیل سرشک عکس رخسارش دید
نقش عجبی بر آب زد آخر کار

ناقوس نواز گر ز من دارد عار
سجاده نشین اگر ز من کرده کنار
من نیز به رغم هر دو انداخته‌ام
تسبیح در آتش، آتش اندر زنار

یا رب بگشا گره ز کار من زار
رحمی که زعقل عاجزم در همه کار
جز در گه تو کی بودم در گاهی
محروم ازین درم مکن یا غفار

102

My eyes could not bear glance at the lover's face;
     tears rained in the presence of that moonlit face.
In the flood of tears I saw the face of the lover:
     wondrous picture she drew on the undulant sea![37]

103

If the sexton is shamed by my presence,
     if the prayer rug avoids my bearing,[38]
I, too, have abandoned them, have
     tossed my prayer beads in the fire, fire in the Zonár.

104

O Lord! Untie the knots in my worthless life.
     Mercy, O God! I lack sufficient thoughts.
But for your door, where could I turn?
     O Merciful Lord! Do not deny me your door.

گفتم: چشمم، گفت: براهش میدار
گفتم: جگرم، گفت: پر آهش میدار
گفتم که: دلم، گفت: چه داری در دل
گفتم: غم تو، گفت: نگاهش میدار

با یار موافق آشنایی خوشتر
وز همدم بی‌وفا جدایی خوشتر
چون سلطنت زمانه بگذاشتنیست
پیوند به ملک بینوایی خوشتر

گر دور فتادم از وصالت به ضرور
دارد دلم از یاد تو صد نوع حضور
خاصیت سایهٔ تو دارم که مدام
نزدیک توام اگر چه می‌افتم دور

105

I said, "My eyes"—she said, "Keep 'em on road."
      I said, "My heart"—she said, "Fill it with sighs."
I said, "My heart"—she said, "What you hide in there?"
      I replied, "Love's Woes"—she advised, "Keep it in there!"

106

With faithful companion, closeness is best;
      with a faithless friend, separation is best.
Since the kingship of the times is transitory,
      connecting to the kingdom of poverty is best.

107

Fate deprives me of your presence;
      yet my heart recalls a thousand of your presence.
Like a shadow, constantly following,
      near you staying, yet behind you tracking.

۱۰۸

در بارگه جلالت ای عذر پذیر
دریاب که من آمده‌ام زار و حقیر
از تو همه رحمتست و از من تقصیر
من هیچ نیم همه تویی دستم گیر

۱۰۹

در بزم تو ای شوخ منم زار و اسیر
وز کشتن من هیچ نداری تقصیر
با غیر سخن گویی کز رشک بسوز
سویم نکنی نگه که از غصه بمیر

۱۱۰

مجنون و پریشان توام دستم گیر
سرگشته و حیران توام دستم گیر
هر بی سر و پا چو دستگیری دارد
من بی سر و سامان توام دستم گیر

108

In your glorious court, O Redeemer of sins
        receive me—humbly I come, mournful.
Mercy is You, I, all blames—
        I, nothing; You, perfection—take my hand.

109

You're all festive in the party, I miserable and slaved,
        though you're blameless of my slaughter!
You talk to others, hinting, "Burn in jealous rage!"
        You never look my way, flirting, "Die of woes!"

110

Lover! I'm your mad—pray, your hand, please!
        Wandering lands for your sake, your hand please!
Any pauper has a master who proffers his hand—please:
        I'm homeless, indigent, your hand, please!

ای فضل تو دستگیر من، دستم گیر
سیر آمده‌ام ز خویشتن، دستم گیر
تا چند کنم توبه و تا کی شکنم
ای توبه ده و توبه شکن، دستم گیر

تا روی ترا بدیدم ای شمع تراز
نی کار کنم نه روزه دارم نه نماز
چون با تو بوم مجاز من جمله نماز
چون بی تو بوم نماز من جمله مجاز

در خدمت تو چو صرف شد عمر دراز
گفتم که مگر با تو شوم محرم راز
کی دانستم که بعد چندین تک و تاز
در تو نرسم وز دو جهان مانم باز

111

Your Wisdom, my solace, hold to my hand;
     I am weary of me, hold to my hand.
I am penitent—then I break it;
     Giver-and-Breaker[39] of penitence, hold to my hand.

112

Since seeing your face, O metaphoric candle,
     I cannot work, fast, or pray.
With you present, the license is all prayer;
     in your absence, my prayer is all but license.[40]

113

A life long in your service
     you'd think us sharers of love.
Alas! I gathered after search and rush
     I could never reach you—both worlds lost.[41]

گر چشم تو در مقام ناز آید باز
بیمار تو بر سر نیاز آید باز
ور حسن تو یک جلوه کند بر عارف
از راه حقیقت به مجاز آید باز

دانی که مرا یار چه گفتست امروز
جز ما به کسی در منگر دیده بدوز
از چهره خویش آتشی افروزد
یعنی که بیا و در ره دوست بسوز

دل خسته و جان فگار و مژگان خونریز
رفتم بر آن یار و مه مهرانگیز
من جای نکرده گرم گردون به ستیز
زد بانگ که هان چند نشینی برخیز

114

A blink of your flirting eyes:
>anon, the patient stirs in need!

One glance at your beauty
>the pious man reverts: from trope to truth.

115

My lover, she said with a rage,
>"But me: dare not look at anyone!"

She sent a fire from her gaze, saying,
>"Come—burn in the cause of the friend!"

116

Heavy of heart, body scarred, eyes raining red,
>I went to my lover, the center of my universe!

Barely warming my seat, in anger
>she cried, "What! Sitting down—you better up!"

الله، به فریاد من بی کس رس
فضل و کرمت یار من بی کس بس
هر کس به کسی و حضرتی مینازد
جز حضرت تو ندارد این بی کس کس

نوروز شد و جهان برآورد نفس
حاصل زبهار عمر ما را غم و بس
از قافلهٔ بهار نامد آواز
تا لاله به باغ سر نگون ساخت جرس

دارم دلکی غمین بیامرز و مپرس
صد واقعه در کمین بیامرز و مپرس
شرمنده شوم اگر بپرسی عملم
یا اکرماکرمین بیامرز و مپرس

117

O God, hear me, the cries of a desolate man:
>   your grace and mercy suffice this desolate man.
Any can boast of a mentor—a majesty:
>   your Majesty is what holds this desolate man.

118

Nowruz[42] arrives, nature breathes for life.
>   For me yet, it's woes alone in my life.
The caravan of the spring does not sound
>   until the tulip makes a bell—upside down.[43]

119

Woes break my heart—forgive and do not ask!
>   A thousand events waylay—forgive and do not ask.
Shame will melt me if you ask of my deeds:
>   O Mercy of all Mercies, forgive me and do not ask!

۱۲۰

شاها ز دعای مرد آگاه بترس
وز سوز دل و آه سحرگاه بترس
بر لشکر و بر سپاه خود غره مشو
از آمدن سیل به ناگاه بترس

۱۲۱

ای آینهٔ ذات تو ذات همه کس
مرآت صفات تو صفات همه کس
ضامن شدم از بهر نجات همه کس
بر من بنویس سیات همه کس

۱۲۲

دل جای تو شد و گر نه پر خون کنمش
در دیده تویی و گر نه جیحون کنمش
امید وصال تست جان را ورنه
از تن به هزار حیله بیرون کنمش

120

O king, beware of the discerning man's prayer;
      beware of the dawn's heartbreaking sighs.
Boasting of your armies and ranks?
      beware of sudden deluge of the floods!

121

The mirror of Your nature, the nature of all,
      the mirror of Your merits, the merit of all.
I've guaranteed the redemption of all:
      debit me the guilt of all.[44]

122

My heart, your seat: else, I would've filled it with blood;
      my eyes, your place: otherwise, Jeyhun[45] would flood.
The hope of union keeps my soul glowing:
      otherwise, my ghost would've folded its tent last night!

آتش بدو دست خویش بر خرمن خویش
چون خود زده‌ام چه نالم از دشمن خویش
کس دشمن من نیست منم دشمن خویش
ای وای من و دست من و دامن خویش

پیوسته مرا ز خالق جسم و عرض
حقا که همین بود و همینست غرض
کان جسم لطیف را به خلوتگه ناز
فارغ بینم همیشه ز آسیب مرض

ای بر سر حرف این و آن نازده خط
پندار دویی دلیل بعدست بخط
در جملهٔ کاینات بی سهو و غلط
یک عین فحسب دان و یک ذات فقط

123

With mine own hands, I've set my harvest afire:
  I've done it: I cannot blame it on my foes!
No one is my enemy but myself!
  O, alas me, my hand—and, my judgment!

124

God married my body to my infirmities:
  the very intent of His art.
The delicate soul in its insular haunt,
  freed from ravenous harm.

125

You, who haven't cancelled a word of this—or that:
  a second thought, remoter reason for that line.
In the sentence of the universe, without error or mistake
  take an 'yen for body and only a zát for soul.[46]

بر عود دلم نواخت یک زمزمه عشق
زان زمزمه‌ام ز پای تا سر همه عشق
حقا که به عهدها نیایم بیرون
از عهدهٔ حق گزاری یک دمه عشق

خلقان همه بر درگهت ای خالق پاک
هستند پی قطرهٔ آبی غمناک
سقای سحاب را بفرما از لطف
تا آب زند بر سر این مشتی خاک

دامان غنای عشق پاک آمد پاک
زآلودگی نیاز با مشتی خاک
چون جلوه گر و نظارگی جمله خود اوست
گر ما و تو در میان نباشیم چه باک

126

She plays her air on my heart, her lute;
      Head to toe she fills me with her tune.
Rightly, I cannot leave, ever,
      the trust of that moment's loving.

127

O Creator, your creatures at your door,
      begging in sorrow for a single droplet of water.
Order your heavenly clouds to rain
      a few driblets on this handful of dust!

128

The treasure of love flows pure,
      from demands of need, cleansed by a handful of dust.
The Observer and the Observed, He Himself:
      if you and I are not present, so, what of it?

بر چهره ندارم زمسلمانی رنگ
بر من دارد شرف سگ اهل فرنگ
آن رو سیهم که باشد از بودن من
دوزخ را ننگ و اهل دوزخ را ننگ

تا شیر بدم شکار من بود پلنگ
پیروز شدم به هرچه کردم آهنگ
تا عشق ترا به بر درآوردم تنگ
از بیشه برون کرد مرا روبه لنگ

دستی که زدی به ناز در زلف تو چنگ
چشمی که زدیدنت زدل بردی زنگ
آن چشم ببست بی توام دیده به خون
و آن دست بکوفت بی توام سینه به سنگ

129

My face shows no color of Islam,
      honors a Ferangi[47] dog more than myself.
My face—disgraced by my self—offends
      the hell and its denizens with shame.

130

A lion, my prey was tiger!
      Victorious in all my adventures!
I gathered your love tightly to my heart:
      Now I limp out of the forest—a mere mouse!

131

My hand—tenderly playing with your hair,
      my eye—draining my heart at your sight.
Without you my eye is dimmed in blood,
      my hand beating my breast with rock.

پرسید کسی منزل آن مهر گسل
گفتم که: دل منست او را منزل
گفتا که: دلت کجاست؟ گفتم: بر او
پرسید که: او کجاست؟ گفتم: در دل

درماند کسی که بست در خوبان دل
وز مهر بتان نگشت پیوند گسل
در صورت گل معنی جان دید و بماند
پای دل او تا به قیامت در گل

شیدای ترا روح مقدس منزل
سودای ترا عقل مجرد محمل
سیاح جهان معرفت یعنی دل
در بحر غمت دست به سر پای به گل

Someone asked about her home;
   I said, "It's my heart, her home."
He asked, "Where is your heart?" I said, "With her."
   He asked, "Where is she?" I said, "In my heart!"

Powerless he, who yields his heart to a face:
   does not remove his love from the idol face!
In the face of the petal he sees the meaning of soul:
   his foot caught in the mud till comes the Resurrection!

Your love-madness indwells in Holy Ghost,
   your affairs carried by the One Wisdom.
The wayfarer of the universe is heart
   Yearning:[48] hand on his head, feet in mud.

می‌رست زدشت خاوران لالهٔ آل
چون دانهٔ اشک عاشقان در مه و سال
بنمود چو روی دوست از پرده جمال
چون صورت حال من شدش صورت حال

هر جا که وجود کرده سیرست ای دل
می‌دان به یقین که محض خیرست ای دل
هر شر ز عدم بود، عدم غیر وجود
پس شر همه مقتضای غیرست ای دل

در عشق چه به ز بردباری ای دل
گویم به تو یک سخن زیاری ای دل
هر چند رسد ز یار خواری ای دل
زنهار به روی او نیاری ای دل

135

From the east, in the plains the tulip bowed
        like the drops of a lover's tear in months and years.
When the beloved's face revealed from its veil,
        When the veil slipped from the beloved's face.

136

O my heart, whenever she roams
        surely, it's for a graceful end.
Sin is a lack, and she has none such:
        only the others bear it!

137

In love, patience is best—
        helpful advice you must heed.
By a lover if neglected: beware!
        Never confront a lover with that.

۱۳۸

با خود در وصل تو گشودن مشکل
دل را به فراق آزمودن مشکل
مشکل حالی و طرفه مشکل حالی
بودن مشکل با تو، نبودن مشکل

۱۳۹

با اهل زمانه آشنایی مشکل
با چرخ کهن ستیزه رایی مشکل
از جان و جهان قطع نمودن آسان
در هم زدن دل به جدایی مشکل

۱۴۰

رنجورم و در دل از تو دارم صد غم
بی لعل لبت حریف دردم همه دم
زین عمر ملولم من مسکین غریب
خواهد شود آرامگهم کوی عدم

138

With you, my love, our union is difficult:
      teaching my heart to accept separation, difficult.
You're the difficulty of my life, its novelty, yet:
      being with you is difficult, away from you, difficult.

139

Fellowship with the people of our times—it's impossible:
      fighting against the old wheel:[49] impossible.
Easier to cut from this world—and this life:
      valediction afflicting our hearts—it is impossible!

140

Afflicted, a thousand blames in my heart:
      your ruby lips missing, woe is my lot.
Wearied of life, indigent poor:
      I think my resting place in nada!

گر پاره کنی مرا ز سر تا به قدم
موجود شوم ز عشق تو من ز عدم
جانی دارم ز عشق تو کرده رقم
خواهیش به شادی کش و خواهیش به غم

من دانگی و نیم داشتم حبهٔ کم
دو کوزه نبید خریدهام پارهٔ کم
بر بربط ما نه زیر ماندست و نه بم
تا کی گویی قلندری و غم و غم

هم در ره معرفت بسی تاختهام
هم در صف عالمان سر انداختهام
چون پرده ز پیش خویش برداشتهام
بشناختهام که هیچ نشناختهام

141

If my body is torn, limb by limb,

     your love will resurrect it into life.

My being fashioned by your love, now

     choose: murder me in sadness or with love.

142

I possessed one-sixth-and-a-half—perhaps, a whit less![50]

     I've bought two jugs of wine—perhaps, a dram less!

Our harp plays no base—or sharp:

     How long, friend, the talk of ghalandari and your woes?[51]

143

In the path of wisdom I've galloped my thoughts;

     among the ranks of the learned I've bowed my head.

When I pulled the curtain from my face,

     I understood also that I've nothing understood.

حک کردنی است آنچه بنگاشته‌ام
افگندنی است آنچه برداشته‌ام
باطل بودست آنچه پنداشته‌ام
حاصل که به هرزه عمر بگذاشته‌ام

دیریست که تیر فقر را آماجم
بر طارم افلاک فلاکت تاجم
یک شمه ز مفلسی خود برگویم
چندانکه خدا غنیست من محتاجم

هر چند به صورت از تو دور افتادم
زنهار مبر ظن که شدی از یادم
در کوی وفای تو اگر خاک شوم
زانجا نتواند که رباید بادم

144

Obliterate whatever I've painted;
>   toss to the ground whatever I have lifted.
All void and null whatever I have thought:
>   simply put: my life in vanity I've wasted.

145

Of late, the arrow of poverty has marked me:
>   the crest to the dome of the house of afflictions I ride.
A short story of my poverty I tell:
>   God is without needs—I is/am!

146

If absent from your sight,
>   think not erased from my heart.
Like loyal dust spread on your path,
>   no wind dare sweep it from land.

۱۴۷

تا چند به گرد سر ایمان گردم
وقتست کز افعال پشیمان گردم
خاکم ز کلیسیا و آبم ز شراب
کافرتر از آنم که مسلمان گردم

۱۴۸

عودم چو نبود چوب بید آوردم
روی سیه و موی سپید آوردم
چون خود گفتی که ناامیدی کفرست
فرمان تو بردم و امید آوردم

۱۴۹

اندر طلب یار چو مردانه شدم
اول قدم از وجود بیگانه شدم
او علم نمی‌شنید لب بر بستم
او عقل نمی‌خرید دیوانه شدم

147

I walk around the issue of my conviction:
        I deem it time to repent of my deeds!
My dust from the church, my draught from wine,
        alas, I'm too much of a heathen to become a Moslem!

148

I had no Aloe,[52] I chose willow wood,
        my cover in sackcloth and ashes.[53]
You commanded, "Lack of dreams[54] is sin."
        I heard you and found dreams.

149

In pursuit of the lover I felt bold,
        took a step, anon was estranged from my self!
She did not hear Wisdom, and I fell silent;
        she would not listen to reason, I went witless.

۱۵۰

آنان که به نام نیک می‌خوانندم
احوال درون بد نمی‌دانندم
گز زانکه درون برون بگردانندم
مستوجب آنم که بسوزانندم

۱۵۱

عمری به هوس باد هوی پیمودم
در هر کاری خون جگر پالودم
در هر چه زدم دست زغم فرسودم
دست از همه باز داشتم آسودم

۱۵۲

در کوی تو من سوخته دامن بودم
وز آتش غم سوخته خرمن بودم
آری جانا دوش به بامت بودم
گفتی دزدست دزد نبد من بودم

150

Those who remember me with kind words
      do not know the evil inside me.
If seen me inside out,
      agreed: I'm fit to be burned.

151

In lust I consumed my life:
      in tasks, I spilled my veins.
Weary of my woes,
      I let go of tasks—I'm in peace.

152

In your alley, I was desolate, aflame,
      my sore heart with woes afire.
It was I at your door, not a thief:
      but you mistook my heart for a thief!

یک چند دویدم و قدم فرسودم
آخر بی تو پدید نامد سودم
تا دست به بیعت وفایت سودم
در خانه نشستم و فرو آسودم

ز آمیزش جان و تن تویی مقصودم
وز مردن و زیستن تویی مقصودم
تو دیر بزی که من برفتم ز میان
گر من گویم، ز من تویی مقصودم

در خواب جمال یار خود میدیدم
وز باغ وصال او گلی می‌چیدم
مرغ سحری زخواب بیدارم کرد
ای کاش که بیدار نمی‌گردیدم

153

A while, I rushed and wore myself thin!
      I saw at last: without you no profit came.
My melancholy sought your hand:
      failing, I stayed home—I'm rested!

154

My Soul and my body, you are my purpose;
      life and death, you, my purpose.
"Long life to you: I am dying,"
      I say. "For me, you're my purpose."

155

In my sleep I was dreaming of the face of my love:
      in our union I was picking a beautiful flower.
The morning bird, alas, me awakened:
      from my dream I wished I had never awakened.

روزی ز پی گلاب می‌گردیدم
پژمرده عذار گل در آتش دیدم
گفتم که چه کرده‌ای که میسوزندت
گفتا که درین باغ دمی خندیدم

دیشب که بکوی یار می‌گردیدم
دانی که پی چه کار می‌گردیدم
قربان خلاف وعده‌اش می‌گشتم
گرد سر انتظار می‌گردیدم

گر در سفرم تویی رفیق سفرم
ور در حضرم تویی انیس حضرم
القصه بهر کجا که باشد گذرم
جز تو نبود هیچ کسی در نظرم

156

I was looking for a measure of rose water
        and saw the withering face of the rose in fire.
I asked, "What sin to deserve such burning?"
        Replied, "Just so! I smiled for a moment in the garden!"[55]

157

Last night, when I walked the lover's lane,
        did you know of my intentions?
I was looking for your broken promise;
        I was after my stolen expectations.

158

In my travels, you are my mate;
        at home, you're my match.
Wherever I happen to pass
        no one but you is in my sight.

یا رب چو به وحدتت یقین می‌دارم
ایمان به تو عالم آفرین می‌دارم
دارم لب خشک و دیدهٔ تر بپذیر
کز خشک و تر جهان همین می‌دارم

از هجر تو ای نگار اندر نارم
می‌سوزم ازین درد و دم اندر نرم
تا دست به گردن تو اندر نرم
آغشته به خون چو دانه اندر نارم

از خاک درت رخت اقامت نبرم
وز دست غمت جان به سلامت نبرم
بردار نقاب از رخ و بنمای جمال
تا حسرت آن رخ به قیامت نبرم

Oh, God, since I confess to your Unity,
> believe in your creation of the universe,
please accept my parched lips and dampened eyes:
> of the wealth in the universe this is the total I hold.[56]

My love—you're absent, I'm in hell—!
> though I burn, I will complain to no one.
Unless I wrap my arms around your waist,
> a seed I remain, bloodied in a pomegranate.[57]

I will not cease my vigil at your door;
> I'll have no respite from the sorrow in my heart.
Remove that veil; reveal that beauteous face:
> do not postpone my hope until the doomsday.

آزرده ترم گر چه کم آزار ترم
بی یار ترم گر چه وفادار ترم
با هر که وفا و صبر من کردم بیش
سبحان الله به چشم او خوارترم

جهدی بکنم که دل زجان برگیرم
راه سر کوی دلستان برگیرم
چون پرده میان من و دلدار منم
برخیزم و خود را ز میان برگیرم

ساقی اگرم می ندهی می‌میرم
ور ساغر می ز کف نهی می‌میرم
پیمانهٔ هر که پر شود می‌میرد
پیمانهٔ من چو شد تهی می‌میرم

162

I'm tormented, but never torment;
    friendless, yet—I am steadfast:
To whom I bear affection and submission,
    blessed God, in his eyes I am despised!

163

I'll try and be resolute in my heart:
    I'll roam the alley where my love lives.
I'm the curtain between me and love:
    I'll stand up—and draw myself!

164

Saghi,[58] if you refuse me wine, I die:
    if you put the wine jug down, I die.
The wine cup, when full, people die:
    when my cup is empty, I die![59]

نه از سر کار با خلل می‌ترسم
نه نیز ز تقصیر عمل می‌ترسم
ترسم ز گناه نیست آمرزش هست
از سابقهٔ روز ازل می‌ترسم

مشهود و خفی چو گنج دقیانوسم
پیدا و نهان چو شمع در فانوسم
القصه درین چمن چو بید مجنون
می‌بالم و در ترقی معکوسم

عیبم مکن ای خواجه اگر می نوشم
در عاشقی و باده پرستی کوشم
تا هشیارم نشسته با اغیارم
چون بی‌هوشم به یار هم آغوشم

165

From the start I had no fear of hurts;
      I never feared the consequences of my deeds.
My fear is not of commission of sins; forgiveness comes:
      I fear that antecedent—immortality![60]

166

Obvious or hid, I'm an ancient treasure;
      seen or veiled, like a candle I'm in a lantern.
In this meadow like a weeping willow
      I boast and am in a reverse spiral!

167

Sir, do not scold me if I indulge in wine:
      I simply engage in making love and drinking wine!
Sober, I sit with my dull companions:
      ah, besotted—I'm embracing my sweetest love.

از جملهٔ دردهای بی درمانم
وز جملهٔ سوز داغ بی پایانم
سوزنده‌تر آنست که چون مردم چشم
در چشم منی و دیدنت نتوانم

زان دم که قرین محنت وافغانم
هر لحظه ز هجران به لب آید جانم
محروم ز خاک آستانت زانم
کز سیل سرشک خود گذر نتوانم

رویت بینم چو چشم را باز کنم
تن دل شودم چو با تویی راز کنم
جز نام تو پاسخ ندهد هیچ کسی
هر جا که به نام خلق آواز کنم

168

Of all the incurable pains—
        the endless burning scars—
Foremost is the pain of knowing, like the iris
        you're in my eye, but I cannot see you!

169

Nearer affliction and wailing
        I fear for my life away from your lips.
I'm robbed of sweeping the dirt at your door:
        tear-flood forbids my crossing the river!

170

I open my eyes, I see your face:
        my body becomes my heart with your words.
But for your name, there is no answer
        when I call in the public gatherings.

بی روی تو رای استقامت نکنم
کس را به هوای تو ملامت نکنم
در جستن وصل تو اقامت نکنم
از عشق تو توبه تا قیامت نکنم

از بیم رقیب طوف کویت نکنم
وز طعنهٔ خلق گفتگویت نکنم
لب بستم و از پای نشستم اما
این نتوانم که آرزویت نکنم

با چشم تو یاد نرگس‌تر نکنم
بی‌لعل تو آرزوی کوثر نکنم
گر خضر به من بی تو دهد آب حیات
کافر باشم که بی تو لب تر نکنم

171

I have no desire to stay without you present;
      I'll not blame anyone for my desiring your presence;
I will not cease seeking our union:
      I will not repent of your love—to the very edge of doom!

172

Fearing rivals, I quit visiting your home;
      weary of tongues, I ceased my praise of you:
I closed my lips and stayed my legs, but
      I cannot do this: kill my desire of your love!

173

Your eyes, how can I think of narcissus?[61]
      Without your lips, I do not desire the waters of Kosar.[62]
Without you if Khezr[63] gifts me the water of eternal life,
      I'll remain a heathen and will refuse to wet my lips.

با درد تو اندیشهٔ درمان نکنم
با زلف تو آرزوی ایمان نکنم
جانا تو اگر جان طلبی خوش باشد
اندیشهٔ جان برای جانان نکنم

عشق تو ز خاص و عام پنهان چه کنم
دردی که ز حد گذشت درمان چه کنم
خواهم که دلم به دیگری میل کند
من خواهم و دل نخواهد ای جان چه کنم

یادت کنم ار شاد و اگر غمگینم
نامت برم ار خیزم اگر بنشینم
با یاد تو خو کردهام ای دوست چنانک
در هرچه نظر کنم ترا میبینم

174

Your pain in my heart, I will not seek remedy!
      With your hair flowing—I cannot hope for faith!
My Life, if you demand my life—it's splendid!
      I'll not think twice of my life for my Life.[64]

175

Why conceal my love from kin and stranger?
      How can I heal my pain past limits?
I wished my heart inclined to another:
      but it's my wish—not heart's; what profits?

176

If happy or sad, I remember your face;
      standing or sitting, I whisper your name.
So attuned to your memory, my friend,
      at whatever I glance, I see your face.

آن بخت ندارم که به کامت بینم
یا در گذری هم به سلامت بینم
وصل تو بهیچگونه دستم ناید
نامت بنویسم و به نامت بینم

غمناکم و از کوی تو با غم نروم
جز شاد و امیدوار و خرم نروم
از درگه همچو تو کریمی هرگز
نومید کسی نرفت و من هم نروم

یا رب تو چنان کن که پریشان نشوم
محتاج برادران و خویشان نشوم
بی منت خلق خود مرا روزی ده
تا از در تو بر در ایشان نشوم

177

In the stars I do not see us united,
        nor see you walk—safely about your way.
Our union, an impossible fare:
        your name I'll pen—see you—in the name!

178

In sorrow, but I will not leave you with grief,
        will not leave except with gladness of dreams.
From your doorway, generous man,
        no one has ever left hopeless—nor will I.

179

O God, settle that I am not wearied,
        dependent on my neighbor and kin.
Give me your grace, give the gift of my bread:
        I will not leave your door for their door.

۱۸۰

جانا من و تو نمونهٔ پرگاریم
سر گر چه دو کرده‌ایم یک تن داریم
بر نقطه روانیم کنون چون پرگار
در آخر کار سر بهم باز آریم

۱۸۱

هیهات که باز بوی می می‌شنوم
آوازهٔ های و هوی و هی می‌شنوم
از گوش دلم سر الهی هر دم
حق میگوید ولی ز نی می‌شنوم

۱۸۲

نی باغ به بستان نه چمن می‌خواهم
نی سرو و نه گل نه یاسمن می‌خواهم
خواهم زخدای خویش کنجی که در آن
من باشم و آن کسی که من می‌خواهم

180

You and I, my love, are a pair of compasses;
      though divided in twain, in body we are one.
We circle on a point, anon like compasses
      at the end, we bring our heads together as one.[65]

181

Alas, again I smell the taste of wine;
      I hear happy and moaning song.
In my heart's ear divine secrets God reveals,
      but I hear only the song from that harp.

182

Not a garden, not land, nor a meadow—
      I decline all—no willow, rose, or a jasmine bush.
A corner I request from my God,
      where I could sit—with my thou!

دارم ز خدا خواهش جنات نعیم
زاهد به ثواب و من به امید عظیم
من دست تهی میروم او تحفه بهِ دست
تا زین دو کدام خوش کند طبع کریم

دی تازه گلی ز گلشن آورد نسیم
کز نکهت آن مشام جان یافت شمیم
نی نی غلطم که صفحهای بود از سیم
مشکین رقمش معطر از خلق کریم

چون دایره ما ز پوست پوشان توایم
در دایرهٔ حلقه بگوشان توایم
گر بنوازی زجان خروشان توایم
ور ننوازی هم از خموشان توایم

183

I beg of God for my presence in Paradise:
  the hermit for his good deeds, I, for my hopes.
To him I go empty-handed, the hermit with gifts:
  of the two, who pleases the nature of Benefactor?

184

From the garden Zephyr fetched a nascent rose:
  from its scent my savoring came into a new life.
No, no! It's wrong! It was a page of silver:
  its musky imprint stronger than its ample nature!

185

Like a tambourine, I'm your skin wearer;[66]
  in the circle I wear your earrings.[67]
If played, I resonate from my heart;
  if you stay, I'm your silent servant.[68]

هر چند زکار خود خبردار نه‌ایم
بیهوده تماشاگر گلزار نه‌ایم
بر حاشیهٔ کتاب چون نقطهٔ شک
بی کارنه‌ایم اگر چه در کار نه‌ایم

افسوس که ما عاقبت اندیش نه‌ایم
داریم لباس فقر و درویش نه‌ایم
این کبر و منی جمله از آنست که ما
قانع به نصیب و قسمت خویش نه‌ایم

با یاد تو با دیدهٔ تر می‌آییم
وز بادهٔ شوق بی‌خبر می‌آییم
ایام فراق چون به سرآمده‌است
من نیز به سوی تو به سر می‌آییم

186

Although oblivious to my own affairs,
  I'm not idly a watcher of the meadow:
In the margin of the book, like a dot of doubt,
  not idle, although not a part of the affair.

187

Alas, I lack prescience:
  not a Dervish, yet wear worn clothes.[69]
This pride, this boasting is from
  my discontent with my allotted lot!

188

Your memory, and I come with crying eyes;
  I come ignorant of the wine of desires.
The time of separation has come to a head:
  I, too, come to you with my head!

هر چند که دل به وصل شادان کردیم
دیدیم که خاطرت پریشان کردیم
خوش باش که ما خوی به هجران کردیم
بر خود دشوار و بر تو آسان کردیم

ما طی بساط ملک هستی کردیم
بی نقض خودی خداپرستی کردیم
بر ما می وصل نیک می‌پیوندد
تف بر رخ می که زود مستی کردیم

ما با می و مستی سر تقوی داریم
دنیی طلبیم و میل عقبی داریم
کی دنیی و دین هر دو بهم آید راست
اینست که ما نه دین نه دنیی داریم

189

I delighted in our union, yet
     I see it distresses your heart.
Rejoice! I'm acquainted with separations!
     Hard on myself, I make it easy on your self!

190

I peddled my worldly wares,
     worshipped God, not denying myself.
The wine of this union suited me fine.
     Curses: the wine quickly tippled me fast!

191

I intend to forsake wine and tippling:
     I want this world, yet desire the other.
Alas! The twain shall never meet together:
     I hold neither this world nor the other.

شمعم که همه نهان فرو می‌گریم
می‌خندم و هر زمان فرو می‌گریم
چون هیچ کس از گریه من آگه نیست
خوش خوش بمیان جان فرو می‌گریم

در مصطبها درد کشان ما باشیم
بدنامی را نام و نشان ما باشیم
از بد بترانی که تو شان می‌بینی
چون نیک ببینی بدشان ما باشیم

ببرید ز من نگار هم خانگیم
بدرید به تن لباس فرزانگیم
مجنون به نصیحت دلم آمده‌است
بنگر به کجا رسیده دیوانگیم

192

I'm a candle, crying, hid from prying eyes;
     I laugh, but in secret my eyes crying.
Not a soul knows of my closet weeping:
     willingly I cry from my inner depths.

193

At the bench[70] in the tavern, lees drinker, I am:
     the sign of disgrace squarely at my feet.
You glimpse—see glorious dignity;
     look closer! You'll find abating dignity.

194

My love, my housemate—she left,
     ripped the garment of my prudence off.
Now, Majnun[71] has come to my counsel:
     observe the circles of my madness!

من لایق عشق و درد عشق تو نیم
زنهار که هم نبرد عشق تو نیم
چون آتش عشق تو بر آرد شعله
من دانم و من که مرد عشق تو نیم

در حضرت پادشاه دوران ماییم
در دایرهٔ وجود سلطان ماییم
منظور خلایقست این سینهٔ ما
پس جام جهان نمای خلقان ماییم

در درویشی هیچ کم و بیش مدان
یک موی تو در تصرف خویش مدان
و آنرا که بود روی به دنیا و به دین
در دوزخ یا بهشت درویش مدان

195

Not worthy of your love, nor the pain;
> for your love, I am not a worthy combatant!

When the fire of your love rains flames,
> only I know I'm not worthy of your love.

196

In the presence of the King of our times, I am:
> in the very being of the Sultan, I am.

My bosom is the object of creations:
> the reflection pool[72] for the created man.

197

If a Dervish, you cannot think of more or less,
> assume you possess even a strand of your hair!

Those who turn to this world—and to religion—
> consider them ná-Dervish[73]—in heaven or in hell.

بگریختم از عشق تو ای سیمین تن
باشد که زغم باز رهم مسکین من
عشق آمد واز نیم رهم باز آورد
مانندهٔ خونیان رسن در گردن

فریاد ز دست فلک بی سر و بن
کاندر بر من نه نو بهشت و نه کهن
با این همه نیز شکر میباید کرد
گر زین بترم کند که گوید که مکن

ای خالق ذوالجلال وحی رحمان
سازندهٔ کارهای بی سامانان
خصمان مرا مطیع من می‌گردان
بی‌رحمان را رحیم من می‌گردان

198

I fled from your love, oh you, beautiful soul,
        to have a respite from my woes, poor my soul.
Love chased, halfway returned me back:
        like a murderer, a rope around my neck!

199

O help! Respite from this measureless Wheel,
        The peddler of neither present nor past.
Yet, I am still to be thankful with grace:
        if I'm treated worse, who will ask?

200

O Glorious God of revelation of Grace,
        Guardian to the afflicted and the poor, I pray:
steer my enemies to kindheartedness;
        fill with compassionate love, the savage.

بحریست وجود جاودان موج زنان
زان بحر ندیده غیر موج اهل جهان
از باطن بحر موج بین گشته عیان
بر ظاهر بحر و بحر در موج نهان

جانست و زبانست زبان دشمن جان
گر جانت بکارست نگه‌دار زبان
شیرین سخنی بگفت شاه صنمان
سر برگ درختست، زبان باد خزان

چندین چه زنی نظاره گرد میدان
اینجا دم اژدهاست و زخم پیلان
تا هر که در آید بنهد او دل و جان
فارغ چه کند گرد سرای سلطان

201

Infinite ocean, the eternal source of the swell:
      of the ocean, man sees nothing but the swell.
Heart-born of the water, the watcher of the swell sees
      the surface of the water, the ocean veiled in the swell.[74]

202

Tongue and life, the tongue, enemy of life:
      hold your tongue, save your life!
A wit once told the king of Idols,
      "Head is leaf on the tree, tongue, autumnal wind!"

203

Imprudent purveying the round of the arena:
      here roam the breath of dragons and elephants' wounds.
Any who dares to come, risks his life—and his heart:
      freedom is rare in the circle of a sultan's court?

رفتم به طبیب و گفتم از درد نهان
گفتا: از غیر دوست بر بند زبان
گفتم که: غذا؟ گفت: همین خون جگر
گفتم: پرهیز؟ گفت: از هر دو جهان

فریاد و فغان که باز در کوی مغان
می‌خواره ز می نه نام یابد نه نشان
زانگونه نهان گشت که بر خلق جهان
گشتست نهان گشتن او نیز نهان

آن دوست که هست عشق او دشمن جان
بر باد همی دهد غمش خرمن جان
من در طلبش دربدر و کوی به کوی
او در دل و کرده دست در گردن جان

204

I went to the healer to tell him of my pain,
      he said, "Except for a friend, hold your tongue."
I asked about food; he said, "Just the blood of your heart!"
      What of abstentions? He cried, "Here—and hereafter!"

205

Again in the tavern-keeper alley
      the drinker finds no trace of wine!
Such a secret! To the drinker
      its concealment is a secret!

206

The friend—her love—the enemy of my life:
      to the wind she scatters the fruit of my life.
I am a vagrant wonderer in her suit:[75]
      she, in my heart, her hands around my neck!

یا رب ز قناعتم توانگر گردان
وز نور یقین دلم منور گردان
روزیِ من سوختهٔ سرگردان
بی منت مخلوق میسر گردان

یا رب زدو کون بی‌نیازم گردان
وز افسر فقر سرفرازم گردان
در راه طلب محرم رازم گردان
زان ره که نه سوی تست بازم گردان

یا رب ز کمال لطف خاصم گردان
واقف بحقایق خواصم گردان
از عقل جفا کار دل افگار شدم
دیوانهٔ خود کن و خلاصم گردان

207

O Lord, enrich me with my frugality;
      light my heart with the fire of surety.
For my daily portion—a dejected wanderer—
      from humankind make my independence tenable!

208

My God! Free me from the needs of the domain:
      with the crown of poverty honor me.
Be my companion in the path of your ways:
      stop me from the path that is not your way.

209

Your Grace, O God, and make me whole:
      aware of the truth by the elect!
Weary of the cruel wisdom,
      release me: make me your mad.

دارم گله از درد نه چندان چندان
با گریه توان گفت نه خندان خندان
در و گهرم جمله بتاراج برفت
آن در و گهر چه بود دندان دندان

دنیا گذران، محنت دنیا گذران
نی بر پدران ماند و نی بر پسران
تا بتوانی عمر به طاعت گذران
بنگر که فلک چه میکند با دگران

بر گوش دلم ز غیب آواز رسان
مرغ دل خسته را به پرواز رسان
یا رب که به دوستی مردان رهت
این گمشدهٔ مرا به من باز رسان

210

I've a grievance with pain—not really so much!

      but it could be told more with a cry, not smile!

All my ivory and pearls are plundered.

      What was that pearl? My teeth—MY TEETH!

211

Sublunary lovers suffer sublunary pain:

      not the father is spared, nor the son.

Obedience and worship are elemental:

      see the Wheel? What has it done to your friends?

212

Sing mystery songs to the ear of my heart:

      wing this desolate heart to flight.

O God, for the love of the men of Your path,

      to me the lost love of mine restore.

قومی که حقست قبلهٔ همتشان
تا سر داری مکش سر از خدمتشان
آنرا که چشیده زهر آفاق زدهر
خاصیت تریاق دهد صحبتشان

فریاد ز شب روی و شب رنگیشان
وز چشم سیاه و صورت زنگیشان
از اول شب تا به دم آخر شب
اینها همه در رقص و منم چنگیشان

رخسار تو بی نقاب دیدن نتوان
دیدار تو بی حجاب دیدن نتوان
مادام که در کمال اشراق بود
سر چشمهٔ آفتاب دیدن نتوان

213

The tribe, those with high-minded purpose:
        never neglect and elude their service.
Those tasting the potion of life dealt by Fortune
        carry in their words the antidote to the poison.

214

God forbid: their faces black as night,
        their black eyes, their Nubian skin.[76]
From the beginning of night to the morning
        they are in dance and I, their harp!

215

Your face, without a veil, invisible;
        a sight of you, without a mask, impossible.
In the perfection of the dazzling light,
        the source of the sun remains invisible.[77]

با گلرخ خویش گفتم: ای غنچه دهان
هر لحظه مپوش چهره چون عشوه دهان
زد خنده که: من بعکس خوبان جهان
در پرده عیان باشم و بی پرده نهان

بنگر به جهان سر الهی پنهان
چون آب حیات در سیاهی پنهان
پیدا آمد ز بحر ماهی انبوه
شد بحر ز انبوهی ماهی پنهان

سودت نکند به خانه در بنشستن
دامنت به دامنم بباید بستن
کان روز که دست ما به دامان تواست
ما را نتوان ز دامنت بگسستن

216

I told my lover, my flower, "Your budding mouth:
>   do not cover your face, like your flirting mouth!"
She said, laughing, "Unlike other beauties of life
>   I'm visible under veil, invisible without a cover!"

217

Look around! The secret of God,
>   like the Well of Life, in darkness veiled.
Masses of fish swirl to the ocean,
>   the ocean by the mass of fish veiled.

218

What profit sitting idly at home:
>   my garment to yours I must tie.
My hands reaching your way,
>   I will find no breach in my way.[78]

پل بر زبر محیط قلزم بستن
راه گردش به چرخ و انجم بستن
نیش و دم مار و دم کژدم بستن
بتوان نتوان دهان مردم بستن

از ساحت دل غبار کثرت رفتن
به زانکه به هرزه در وحدت سفتن
مغرور سخن مشو که توحید خدا
واحد دیدن بود نه واحد گفتن

عشق آن صفتی نیست که بتوان گفتن
وین در به سر الماس نشاید سفتن
سوداست که می‌پزیم والله که عشق
بکر آمد و بکر هم بخواهد رفتن

It's possible to bridge over the Red Sea,
        make our walk follow the course of stars,
Tie the fang and the breath of a snake—scorpion's tail,
        but it's not possible to make people shut their mouths.

220

Sweeping the excessive dust from the plain of heart
        is better than boring the pearl of Oneness in vain.
Be not glory in your words: the Oneness of God
        is a singleness of seeing, not one of words.

221

Love is not love if it's advertised:
        this pearl by a diamond bit must not be holed.
It's only a fancy of trading we cook: God knows
        love is born in tact, intact it goes.

از باده بروی شیخ رنگ آوردن
اسلام ز جانب فرنگ آوردن
ناقوس به کعبه در درنگ آوردن
بتوان نتوان ترا بچنگ آوردن

تا لعل تو دلفروز خواهد بودن
کارم همه آه و سوز خواهد بودن
گفتی که بخانهٔ تو آیم روزی
آن روز کدام روز خواهد بودن

یا رب تو زخواب ناز بیدارش کن
وز مستی حسن خویش هشیارش کن
یا بی‌خبرش کن که نداند خود را
یا آنکه زحال خود خبردارش کن

222

It's possible to bring color to a sheik's visage with wine,
       or import Islam from the lands of the Franks,[79]
Or ring a church bell from the minarets in Kaaba,[80]
       but it's impossible to gain access to my sweetheart!

223

Your lips, as long as they smile,
       our lot will all be sighing and woes.
You said, "I'll come to your house—one day!"
       Pray tell, please: when is that day?

224

O Lord, raise her from her beauty sleep,
       sober her up from the self-praise of her face.
Keep her ignorant, so she doesn't know herself:
       or, make her aware of the state of her self.

یک لحظه چراغ آرزوها پف کن
قطع نظر از جمال هر یوسف کن
زین شهد یک انگشت به کام تو کشم
از لذت اگر مست نگردی تف کن

خواهی که کسی شوی زهستی کم کن
ناخورده شراب وصل مستی کم کن
با زلف بتان دراز دستی کم کن
بت را چه گنه تو بت‌پرستی کم کن

درویشی کن قصد در شاه مکن
وز دامن فقر دست کوتاه مکن
اندر دهن مار شو و مال مجوی
در چاه نشین و طلب جاه مکن

225

For a moment, squelch the light of your desires,
      beautiful face of Joseph,[81] forget.
From this honey to your lips I will rub:
      if not drunk from its taste, spit.[82]

226

To be someone, let go of your self:
      remain sober till you drink of Union Wine.
With the hair of the idols, do not indulge:
      why blame the idol? You, the idolater.

227

Rather be a Dervish—than aim up at the throne,
      disavowing the garments of a fakir.
Rather in the mouth of a python—than ask for opulence;
      rather sit down in a well—than ask for worldly honors.

گفتم که: رخم به رنگ چون کاه مکن
کس را ز من و کار من آگاه مکن
گفتا که: اگر وصال ما می‌طلبی
گر میکشمت دم مزن و آه مکن

یا رب تو به فضل مشکلم آسان کن
از فضل و کرم درد مرا درمان کن
بر من منگر که بی کس و بی هنرم
هر چیز که لایق تو باشد آن کن

ای غم گذری به کوی بدنامان کن
فکر من سرگشتهٔ بی سامان کن
زان ساغر لبریز که پر می ز غمست
یک جرعه به کار بی سرانجامان کن

I begged, "My face, do not pale it—like the moon!"
      Do not tell anyone—my affairs and secrets."
She said, "Lover, if you hope for our union,
      don't breathe or sigh—even if I kill you!"

229

O God, untie the knots in my life—your Grace;
      heal my pain and woes—your Wisdom and Grace
Do not look at me as a lonely vagabond—no arts;
      Let thy will be done.

230

O pain, blow, my way the way of the disgraced:
      remember me, bewildered and homeless.
From the cup of wine, overflowing with woes,
      drink a draught for the indefinite affairs of my life.

رازی که به شب لب تو گوید با من
گفتار زبان نگرددش پیرامن
زان سر به گریبان سخن برنارد
پیراهن حرف تنگ دارد دامن

عاشق من و دیوانه من و شیدا من
شهره من و افسانه من و رسوا من
کافر من و بت پرست من ترسا من
اینها من و صد بار بتر زینها من

سلطان گوید که نقد گنجینهٔ من
صوفی گوید که دلق پشمینهٔ من
عاشق گوید که درد دیرینهٔ من
من دانم و من که چیست در سینهٔ من

231

The secret your lips whisper at night:
>   The words of tongue do not wrap around.
Over that head the collar of word cannot slide:
>   the shirt of words has a tight skirt![83]

232

I'm a lover, I'm mad, I'm lovelorn;
>   I'm famous, I'm a legend, I, disgraced;
I'm heathen, I, an idolater, I'm a Christian;
>   I am all of this—and a thousand times worse!

233

The Sultan thinks, "Cash is my treasure!"
>   The Sufi says, "Coarse wool is my garment."
The lover pines, "Pain is my ancient!"
>   I—only I know what is in my heart.

زد شعله به دل آتش پنهانی من
زاندازه گذشت محنت جانی من
معذورم اگر سخن پریشان افتاد
معلوم شود مگر پریشانی من

شوریده دلی و غصه گردون گردون
گریان چشمی و اشک جیحون جیحون
کاهیده تنی و شعله خرمن خرمن
هر شعله ز کوه قاف افزون افزون

فریاد ز دست فلک آینه گون
کز جور و جفای او جگر دارم خون
روزی به هزار غم به شب می‌آرم
تا خود فلک از پرده‌چه آرد بیرون

234

My hidden fire sets my heart aflame;
  my body pain and woes pass all endurance.
Forgive me if my words lack coherence
  sorry my distress is so apparent!

235

My heart is lovesick,
  eyes, weeping Jeyhun.[84]
I'm diminished, my crops aflame:
  the flames of Gháf[85] ablaze.

236

Alas the echoing wheel of fortune,
  my heart bleeds from its woes.
A thousand woes, I pass my days to nights,
  waiting to see what the wheel unveils?

تا گرد رخ تو سنبل آمد بیرون
صد ناله ز من چون بلبل آمد بیرون
پیوسته ز گل سبزه برون می‌آید
این طرفه که از سبزه گل آمد بیرون

در راه یگانگی نه کفرست و نه دین
یک گام زخود برون نه و راه ببین
ای جان جهان تو راه اسلام گزین
با مار سیه نشین و با ما منشین

گر سقف سپهر گردد آیینهٔ چین
ور تختهٔ فولاد شود روی زمین
از روزی تو کم نشود دان به یقین
میدان که چنینست و چنینست و چنین

237

Her face, hyacinth round:
       I, singing my nightingale song.
Flowers branch all summer long:
       when did this rare flower sprout?

238

In the path of Oneness, there is no sacred or profane:
       take a step ahead of you, see the path.
O you, the soul of the universe, choose Islam:
       sit with the black snake and avoid our band.

239

If the ceiling of the heavens turns into a mirror,
       if the face of earth is paved with a steel shroud,
there cannot be a reduction in your portion:
       you must know! It is such, it is such, and thus!

هر چند که یار سر گرانست به تو
غمگین نشوی که مهربانست به تو
دلدار مثال صورت آینه است
تا تو نگرانی نگرانست به تو

دورم اگر از سعادت خدمت تو
پیوسته دلست آینهٔ طلعت تو
از گرمی آفتاب هجرم چه غمست
دارم چو پناه سایهٔ دولت تو

جان و دل من فدای خاک در تو
گر فرمایی بدیده آیم بر تو
وصلت گوید که تو نداری سرما
بی سر بادا هر که ندارد سر تو

240

Your lover is cross with you?
>   No matter! She will be kind to you.
A lover is like a mirror,
>   echoing back your mood to you.

241

Even if deprived from the grace of serving you,
>   your face remains true in the mirror of my heart.
What care if the heat of the blazing sun reigns:
>   I enjoy the protection of the shade of your Grace.

242

Sweet love, I offer myself as the mat at your door.
>   Order me—and you'll find me at your feet.
A voice inside whispers, "She's not on you keen!"
>   May anyone who is not keen on you lose his head![86]

۲۴۳

ای سبزی سبزهٔ بهاران از تو
وی سرخی روی گل عذاران از تو
آه دل و اشک بی قراران از تو
فریاد که باد از تو و باران از تو

۲۴۴

ای پیر و جوان دهر شاد از غم تو
فارغ دل هیچ کس مباد از غم تو
مسکین من بیچاره درین عالم خاک
سرگردانم چو گرد باد از غم تو

۲۴۵

ای کعبه پرست چیست کین من و تو
صاحب نظرند خرده بین من و تو
گر بر سنجند کفر و دین من و تو
دانند نهایت یقین من و تو

243

You, the emerald source of beauty of leaves,
     the coral-hint on the face of the beautiful belles;
the sighs and tears of mad lovers are your fault:
     alas, you're the source of storms and rains!

244

Young and old, happy to sorrow for your love:
     may no heart live free of woes.
Alas, this beggar, I, on this globe
     wandering rounds like a whirlwind of your woes.

245

You, the Kaaba[87] worshipper! Why this contention?
     Visionary, discerning eyes will see
if our faith and disbelief are compared:
     they will know the extent of our certainty.

درد دل من دواش می‌دانی تو
سوز دل من سزاش می‌دانی تو
من غرق گنه پردهٔ عصیان در پیش
پنهان چه کنم که فاش می‌دانی تو

من میشنوم که می نبخشایی تو
هر جا که شکسته‌ایست آنجایی تو
ما جمله شکستگان درگاه توایم
در حال شکستگان چه فرمایی تو

ما را نبود دلی که کار آید ازو
جز ناله که هر دمی هزار آید ازو
چندان گریم که کوچه‌ها گل گردد
نی روید و ناله‌های زار آید ازو

You know! You hold the balm for my heartache:
      the retribution of the sighs of my woes.
Drowning in sin, the curtain of rebellion in front,
      how can I hide them: You know them all.

I hear, they say, You, the Forgiver:
      you are where there is a broken soul.
We the broken are, come to Your presence:
      what say You about our broken ways?

My heart! Nothing can come out of it
      except groans and sighs, a thousand a minute!
I will cry till the streets turn into mud,
      till reeds grow and make wailing sounds of my woes!

زلفش بکشی شب دراز آید ازو
ور بگذاری چنگل باز آید ازو
ور پیچ و خمش ز یک دگر باز کنی
عالم عالم مشک فراز آید ازو

سودای سر بی سر و سامان یک سو
بی مهری چرخ و دور گردان یکسو
اندیشهٔ خاطر پریشان یک سو
اینها همه یک سو غم جانان یکسو

از هر چه نه از بهر تو کردم توبه
ور بی تو غمی خوردم از آن غم توبه
و آن نیز که بعد ازین برای تو کنم
گر بهتر از آن توان از آن هم توبه

249

Stretch my lover's hair: a long night follows!
    If you allow, her claws show.
Untying the curls and twists from each other:
    showers of musk flow from its rows.

250

Never mind the matter of my confused state,
    the lack of kindness of the wheel of fortune,
the burden of thinking only of memories:
    yes, all these, but the loss of a friend is most.

251

I repent what I have done that wasn't for you,
    the sorrows I have suffered that weren't for you.
And, all that I will do hereafter for you:
    if I can do it better for anyone else, I repent that too.

ای خاک نشین درگه قدر تو ماه
دست هوس از دامن وصلت کوتاه
در کوی تو زان خانه گرفتم که مباد
آزرده شود خیالت از دوری راه

ای زاهد و عابد از تو در ناله و آه
نزدیک تو و دور ترا حال تباه
کس نیست که از دست غمت جان ببرد
آن را به تغافل کشی این را بنگاه

اینک سر کوی دوست اینک سر راه
گر تو نروی روندگان را چه گناه
جامه چه کنی کبود و نیلی و سیاه
دل صاف کن و قبا همی پوش و کلاه

252

The luminous moon, a suitor at your door,
      the hand of caprice, cut short reaching your hand.
I took a lodging next to your home, lest
      your mind is troubled: the distance of way.

253

The ascetic and pious for your love, sorrows and sighs;
      near you or away, their state of mind, corrupted;
No one immune from the cruelty of your woes:
      you kill this one with a neglect, that with a look.

254

Now at the turn to the alley, now on the way to your love;
      if you hesitate, what fault of those willing to pass?
Why worry about a garment: black, green or blue!
      Let your heart shine: wear a ghabá—wear a hat![88]

از بس که شکستم و ببستم توبه
فریاد همی کند ز دستم توبه
دیروز به توبه‌ای شکستم ساغر
و امروز به ساغری شکستم توبه

معمورهٔ دل به علم آراسته به
مطمورهٔ تن ز کینه پیراسته به
از هستی خود هر چه توان کاسته به
هر چیز که غیر تست ناخواسته به

از مردم صد رنگ سیه پوشی به
وز خلق فرومایه فراموشی به
از صحبت ناتمام بی خاصیتان
کنجی و فراغتی و خاموشی به

255

I've made and broken repentance so often:
      cried repentance to heavens for my acts.
Yesterday I broke a wine vessel in repentance.
      Today! I broke my repentance with a vessel of wine.

256

The world of mind, better adorned in wisdom;
      the world of body, better free of vengeance.
The world of wealth, better curtailed and less:
      whatever is not yours, better let rest!

257

Better hide from the men of pretense;[89]
      better forget those, ignoble and base.
The conversation of the virtueless:
      avoidance and silence are best.

زاهد خوشدل که ترک دنیا کرده
می خواره خجل که معصیتها کرده
ترسم که کند امید و بیم و آخر کار
ناکرده چو کرده کرده چون ناکرده

بحریست نه کاهنده نه افزاینده
امواج برو رونده و آینده
عالم چو عبارت از همین امواجست
نبود دو زمان بلکه دو آن پاینده

هجران ترا چو گرم شد هنگامه
بر آتش من قطره فشان از خامه
من رفتم و مرغ روح من پیش تو ماند
تا همچو کبوتر از تو آرد نامه

258

The merry ascetic, renouncing his world,
       the drunk ashamed of his sins:
I fear at last, hope and fear will make
       the ascetic a sinner, the sinner an ascetic![90]

259

An ocean, never increasing or losing:
       waves to it, in and out interminably rolling.
The world is the waves,
       not two rotations, but two eternal, parallel motions.

260

When your absence flames my heart,
       send a penned word to quench my pain.
I'm absent, but the bird of my soul remains
       to fetch like a homing pigeon your words.

دنیا طلبان ز حرص مستند همه
موسی کش و فرعون پرستند همه
هر عهد که با خدای بستند همه
از دوستی حرص شکستند همه

سودا به سرم همچو پلنگ اندر کوه
غم بر سر غم بسان سنگ اندر کوه
دور از وطن خویش و به غربت مانده
چون شیر به دریا و نهنگ اندر کوه

ای غم که حجاب صبر بشکافته‌ای
بی تابی من دیده و برتافته‌ای
شب تیره و یار دور و کس مونس نه
ای هجر بکش که بی‌کسم یافته‌ای

In greed the worldly are besotted:

      they are Moses killers and worshippers of Pharaoh.

The covenants they make with God,

      for greed and gain they break them all.

262

Heart pounding, I, like a tiger on a mountain,

      sorrow piled on woe, layers of stone of a mountain.

Away from my home, stranger in town—misplaced:

      like a lion in the ocean, whale in the mountain.

263

Regret, the veil of my patience you have ripped:

      seeing my pain, becoming bolder.

Dark night, friend absent, no companion in sight,

      O absence slay me! You've found me alone.

دارم صنمی چهره برافروخته‌ای
وز خرمن دهر دیده بر دوخته‌ای
او عاشق دیگری و من عاشق او
پروانه صفت سوخته‌ای سوخته‌ای

من کیستم از خویش به تنگ آمده‌ای
دیوانهٔ با خرد به جنگ آمده‌ای
دوشینه به کوی دوست از رشکم سوخت
نالیدن پای دل به سنگ آمده‌ای

ای خالق ذوالجلال و ای بار خدای
تا چند روم دربدر و جای به جای
یا خانه امید مرا در دربند
یا قفل مهمات مرا دربگشای

264

My love—she is flushed on her face,
>   worldly and groomed by the hand of life!
She, lover of another; I, her devotee:
>   like a moth I burn of her blazing fire!

265

Who am I? But weary of myself!
>   A lunatic, fighting sanity.
Yesternight, in the lover's alley jealousy beset me,
>   my feet aching, my heart hard as a rock!

266

O glorious God, O Creator Lord:
>   how long will I go homeless, wondering?
Either close the door to my house of hopes,
>   or, open the lock to the door of my luck!

زلفت سیمست و مشک را کان گشتی
از بسکه بجستی تو همه آن گشتی
ای آتش تا سرد بدی سوختیم
ای وای از آنروز که سوزان گشتی

در کوی خودم مسکن و ماوا دادی
در بزم وصال خود مرا جا دادی
القصه به صد کرشمه و ناز مرا
عاشق کردی و سر به صحرا دادی

اول همه جام آشنایی دادی
آخر بستم زهر جدایی دادی
چون کشته شدم بگفتی این کشتۀ کیست
داد از تو که داد بیوفایی دادی

267

Your hair: a mine treasure of musk,
> so fierce searching, you're what I aspired.
I burned when your fire was cold;
> God help me the day you are hot!

268

You gave me shelter in your home and lodging,
> included me in the feast of coupling;
with a thousand coyness and a thousand flirtations you beckoned
> me to love, then to wilderness exiling.

269

First, you gave the cup of fulfillment,
> then, the poison of separation.
When thus slain, you said, "Who this body?"
> Judgment, O God! Her gift was deceit!

۲۷۰

ای شاه ولایت دو عالم مددی
بر عجز و پریشانی حالم مددی
ای شیر خدا زود به فریادم رس
جز حضرت تو پیش که نالم مددی

۲۷۱

من کیستم از قید دو عالم فردی
عنقا منشی بلند همت مردی
دیوانهٔ بیخودی بیابان گردی
لبریز محبتی سرا پا دردی

۲۷۲

از چهره همه خانه منقش کردی
وز باده رخان ما چو آتش کردی
شادی و نشاط ما یکی شش کردی
عیشت خوش باد عیش ما خوش کردی

270

O King of the Twain Worlds—help!
>Respite from failures and afflictions—help!
O Lion of God, hear my words, haste:
>whom else can I appeal my case—help![91]

271

Who am I? From the ties of both worlds free:
>phoenix-like,[92] a man of high ambitions.
Mad, beside myself, roaming the desert,
>filled with love, head-to-toe in woes.

272

Your face etched on our hearts,[93]
>your wine giving glow to our face.
You've doubled our joy and our pleasure:
>may your pleasure quadruple.

عشقم دادی ز اهل دردم کردی
از دانش و هوش و عقل فردم کردی
سجاده نشین با وقاری بودم
میخواره و رند و هرزه گردم کردی

ای دیده مرا عاشق یاری کردی
داغم ز رخ لاله عذاری کردی
کاری کردی که هیچ نتوان گفتن
الله الله چه خوب کاری کردی

ای چرخ بسی لیل و نهار آوردی
گه فصل خزان و گه بهار آوردی
مردان جهان را همه بردی به زمین
نامردان را بروی کار آوردی

273

Gift of love, scourge of my peace,
      lured away from wisdom and wits.
Once a graceful man of prayers:
      now a lout, drunkard, and doused in vice.

274

My eyes, you've made me into a lover,
      flushed by the beauty of a tulip face.[94]
How can I explain this transaction?
      By God, it was a wonderful act.

275

Many nights and days to this Wheel, spinning:
      awhile it's Autumn, then again Spring.
The noble of the world have been buried,
      the coward set to rule in their place!

ای کاش مرا به نفت آلایندی
آتش بزدندی و نبخشایندی
در چشم عزیز من نمک سایندی
وز دوست جدا شدن نفرمایندی

دستی نه که از نخل تو چینم ثمری
پایی نه که در کوی تو یابم گذری
چشمی نه که بر خویش بگریم قدری
رویی نه که بر خاک بمالم سحری

گیرم که هزار مصحف از برداری
با آن چه کنی که نفس کافر داری
سر را به زمین چه می نهی بهر نماز
آنرا به زمین بنه که بر سر داری

276

Come, soak my body in oil,
        set me aflame—save my soul.
My eyes, sprinkle with salt, but
        from my lover separate me not.

277

No hands to pick dates from your palm,
        no feet to pass by the alley of your house,
no eyes to cry for myself awhile,
        no face to rub in dust of a day!

278

If a thousand books are in your head:
        what of it if your soul is heathenic?[95]
Why set your head on the ground for prayer?[96]
        Put on the ground the burden that is in your head!

ای شمع نمونه‌ای زسوزم داری
خاموشی و مردن رموزم داری
داری خبر از سوز شب هجرانم
آیا چه خبر ز سوز روزم داری

چون گل بگلاب شسته رویی داری
چون مشک بمی حل شده مویی داری
چون عرصه گه قیامت از انبه خلق
پر آفت و محنت سر کویی داری

ای دل بر دوست تحفه جز جان نبری
دردت چو دهند نام درمان نبری
بی درد ز درد دوست نالان گشتی
خاموش که عرض دردمندان نبری

279

O candle, you feel the fever of my woes—
      know the mystery of my wordless death—
aware of the fiery nights of my separation.
      Tell me? Any news of my flaming days?

280

Like the rose, your face washed in the attar,
      your hair musky, suffused in wine.
Like the plain of resurrection, filled thick with men,
      you have a home fraught with danger and suffering.

281

My heart, take no gift to the friend, but my soul;
      if pained, mention not the cure!
No pain, but the pain of the friend, and you complain?
      Silence! You dishonor those in pain.

ای در سر هر کس از خیالت هوسی
بی یاد تو برنیاید از من نفسی
مفروش مرا بهیچ و آزاد مکن
من خواجه یکی دارم و تو بنده بسی

تا نگذری از جمع به فردی نرسی
تا نگذری از خویش به مردی نرسی
تا در ره دوست بی سر و پا نشوی
بی درد بمانی و به دردی نرسی

گه شانه کش طرهٔ لیلا باشی
گه در سر مجنون همه سودا باشی
گه آینهٔ جمال یوسف گردی
گه آتش خرمن زلیخا باشی

282

Who lives free of your desire in his heart?
      No breath without recollecting your face.
Don't sell me, ever, do not free me:
      one master I have, and you've many slaves.

283

Until you move from the collective, individuation you cannot reach;
      until you let go of ego, maturation you cannot find.
Until on the way to the friend you lose,
      you'll be painless, but never know rapture.

284

For a time, you are the dresser of Leili's hair,
      for a time, the wrecker in the head of Majnun.
For a time, you become the mirror of Joseph's beauty:
      for a time, the fatal flame in Zuleikha's harvest.[97]

مزار دلی را که تو جانش باشی
معشوقهٔ پیدا و نهانش باشی
زان می‌ترسم که از دلازاری تو
دل خون شود و تو در میانش باشی

جان چیست غم و درد و بلا را هدفی
دل چیست درون سینه سوزی و تفی
القصه پی شکست ما بسته صفی
مرگ از طرفی و زندگی از طرفی

بگشود نگار من نقاب از طرفی
برداشت سفیده دم حجاب از طرفی
گر نیست قیامت ز چه رو گشت پدید
ماه از طرفی و آفتاب از طرفی

Do not torment the heart of your soul:
>
> its lover, veiled or apparent.

I fear from your torment
>
> the heart will turn to blood, you inside it!

What is life? A target of pain, sorrow and woes;
>
> what is heart? Inside the breast filled with ache and loss.

Simply put: behind the array of our fall
>
> I see death on one side, life on the other.

My love unveiled her face—to my left;
>
> the morning light lifted her cover—to my right.

If not the day of resurrection, why the moon
>
> has appeared from one side, the sun the other?[98]

ای آنکه به کنهت نرسد ادراکی
کونین به پیش کرمت خاشاکی
از روی کرم اگر ببخشی همه را
بخشیده شود پیش تو مشت خاکی

وصافی خود به رغم حاسد تا کی
ترویج چنین متاع کاسد تا کی
تو معدومی خیال هستی از تو
فاسد باشد خیال فاسد تا کی

ای از تو به باغ هر گلی را رنگی
هر مرغی را زشوق تو آهنگی
با کوه ز اندوه تو رمزی گفتم
برخاست صدای ناله از هر سنگی

288

You, Whose vastness cannot be understood by lore:
      the twain worlds at Your feet—but a mote.
Of your grace if you forgive man,
      forgiven at your feet only a handful of dust.

289

How long your self-praise in the face of your enemy,
      offering such goods in an impoverished market?
Since in nada you live, your thought of existence, vanity!
      How long such conceited thoughts?

290

You're the rainbow to give any garden the colors:
      birds from your love break into a song.
I whispered to the mountain your fable of my woes:
      from each rock rose the sound of wailing!

تا بتوانی بکش به جان بار دلی
می‌کوش که تا شوی ز دل یار دلی
آزار دلی مجو که ناگاه کنی
کار دو جهان در سر آزار دلی

از درد تو نیست چشم خالی ز نمی
هر جا که دلیست شد گرفتار غمی
بیماری تو باعث نابودن ماست
ای باعث عمر ما مبادت المی

حقا که اگر چو مرغ پر داشتمی
روزی ز تو صد بار خبر داشتمی
این واقعه‌ام اگر نبودی در پیش
کی دیده ز دیدار تو برداشتمی

Carry the burden of a person heavy of heart;
      be friend from the bottom of your heart.
Seek not to burden another's heart:
      you'll undo salvation with that hurt.

292

You, the cause of our crying eyes,
      the source of woes in our hearts!
Your affliction, our decimation:
      God forbid it, you, the cause of our lives!

293

If I had the wings of a bird, every day
      a hundred times I would fly about for a news.
Even if the wings are impossible,
      I cannot remove my eyes from your face.

نزدیکان را بیش بود حیرانی
کایشان دانند سیاست سلطانی
ما را به سر چاه بری دست زنی
لاحول کنی و دست بر دل رانی

ما را به سر چاه بری دست زنی
لاحول کنی و شست بر شست زنی
بر ما به ستم همیشه دستی داری
گویی عسسی و شامگه مست زنی

تا چند سخن تراشی و رنده زنی
تا کی به هدف تیر پراکنده زنی
گر یک ورق از علم خموشی خوانی
بسیار بدین گفت و شنوخنده زنی

Your inner circles are perplexed—fully:
      they know well the sultan's revenge.
You take us to the well and clap your hands:[99]
      you praise God, then bring your hand to your heart![100]

You take us to the well and clap,
      you praise God and wash your hands.
With your cruel hand you rule us:
      Drunk at night as if you're an as-as![101]

How long will you spin words and breathe nonsense?
      How long will you shoot arrows in vain and miss?
Read a page from the book of the art of silence:
      you will smile at most of our conversations.

خواهی چو خلیل کعبه بنیاد کنی
و آنرا به نماز و طاعت آباد کنی
روزی دو هزار بنده آزاد کنی
به زان نبود که خاطری شاد کنی

ای آنکه سپهر را پر از ابر کنی
وز لطف نظر به سوی هر گبر کنی
کردند تمام خانه‌های تو خراب
ای خانه خراب تا به کی صبر کنی

تا ترک علایق و عوایق نکنی
یک سجدهٔ شایستهٔ لایق نکنی
حقا که ز دام لات و عزی نرهی
تا ترک خود و جمله خلایق نکنی

Do you want, like Ali, to recreate Kaaba,[102]
       have it flourish in worship and prayers,
and free two thousand slaves a day?
       No, you better make one single soul happy!

You, Who fills the heavens with nourishing rains,
       cast a loving eye upon every Magus:
I say, all Your houses in ruins:
       O You ruinous God: how long will you wait?[103]

Unless you forsake your ties and barriers,
       prostrate yourself and pray in earnest:
you will not escape the snare of glory and hurdles,
       unless you forsake your ego—and the rest.

یا رب در خلق تکیه گاهم نکنی
محتاج گدا و پادشاهم نکنی
موی سیهم سفید کردی به کرم
با موی سفید رو سیاهم نکنی

یاقوت ز دیده ریختم تا چه کنی
در پای غم تو بیختم تا چه کنی
از هر که به تو گریختم سود نکرد
از تو به تو در گریختم تا چه کنی

دنیای دنی پر هوس را چه کنی
آلودهٔ هر ناکس و کس را چه کنی
آن یار طلب کن که ترا باشد و بس
معشوقهٔ صد هزار کس را چه کنی

300

O Lord, free me from dependence on anyone:
　　　No need of help from a king nor a beggar.
Your grace, I have now white hair:
　　　do not let my face turn black.[104]

301

I cried rubies from my eyes: what do you say?
　　　I sifted woes at your feet: what do you say?
From every one I fled to you, no fruits:
　　　I fled from you to you: what do you say?

302

Who needs the base world of lust,
　　　the defiled consort of the ignoble and rich?
Seek a friend who's yours alone:
　　　who needs the lover of ten thousands?

از سادگی و سلیمی و مسکینی
وز سرکشی و تکبر و خود بینی
بر آتش اگر نشانیم بنشینم
بر دیده اگر نشانمت ننشینی

ای دل اگر آن عارض دلجو بینی
ذرات جهان را همه نیکو بینی
در آینه کم نگر که خودبین نشوی
خود آینه شو تا همگی او بینی

میدان فراخ و مرد میدانی نی
مردان جهان چنانکه میدانی نی
در ظاهرشان به اولیا می‌مانند
در باطنشان بوی مسلمانی نی

303

Of simplicity, meekness, and poverty,
  of perversion, pride, and conceit
If you point me, I willingly sit in the fire; but
  if on you I try to set my eyes, you refuse![105]

304

O heart, if you can only know that face of beauty,
  in it at once you'll see the universe.
Look not into mirror, lest you become conceited;
  yourself become the mirror to see a beloved everywhere.

305

Vast arena and men to fit them are rare:[106]
  alas, they belie what you imagine of men.
In appearance they are angels:
  inside, there is no trace of a believer.

تحقیق معانی ز عبارات مجوی
بی رفع قیود و اعتبارات مجوی
خواهی یابی ز علت جهل شفا
قانون نجات از اشارات مجوی

در ظلمت حیرت ار گرفتار شوی
خواهی که ز خواب جهل بیدار شوی
در صدق طلب نجات، زیرا که به صدق
شایستهٔ فیض نور انوار شوی

آمد بر من قاصد آن سرو سهی
آورد بهی تا نبود دست تهی
من هم رخ خود بدان بهی مالیدم
یعنی ز مرض نهاده‌ام رو به بهی

306

One cannot deduce meaning from a phrase
  without breaking ties and credits.
If desiring cure from the cause of ignorance,
  do not seek the state of grace from suspicions.

307

In the darkness of doubts if trapped,
  desiring to awake from ignorance,
In truth seek your salvation,
  worthy of the light of the Grace.

308

Your messenger, sweet love, arrived
  with a gift of a quince, generous act of love.
I rubbed the quince all over my face:
  from illness, now, I move to health.[107]

تا تو هوس خدای از سر ننهی
در هر دو جهان نباشدت روی بهی
ور زانکه به بندگی فرود آری سر
ز اندیشهٔ این و آن بکلی برهی

پاکی و منزهی و بی همتایی
کس را نرسد ملک بدین زیبایی
خلقان همه خفته‌اند و درها بسته
یا رب تو در لطف بما بگشایی

آیینه صفت بدست او نیکویی
زین سوی نموده‌ای ولی زان سویی
او دیده ترا که عین هستی تو اوست
زانش تو ندیده‌ای که عکس اویی

Dismiss the lust of claiming to be God
        to have happiness in this world and the other.
Hang your head down in submission
        to receive respite from the cares of this world.

310

Chastity and innocence—matchless:
        no one owns a more beautiful treasure.
The creatures of God all asleep, doors locked:
        O Lord, open the doors of your grace to our face.

311

Like a mirror in her hand, you're wonderful;
        you show this side, but you're on the other.
She has seen you, your being her exact double;
        you haven't seen her because you're her double.

ای آنکه گشایندهٔ هر بند تویی
بیرون ز عبارت چه و چند تویی
این دولت من بس که منم بندهٔ تو
این عزت من بس که خداوند تویی

الله تویی وز دلم آگاه تویی
درمانده منم دلیل هر راه تویی
گر مورچهای دم زند اندر تک چاه
آگه ز دم مورچه در چاه تویی

ای آنکه به ملک خویش پاینده تویی
وز دامن شب صبح نماینده تویی
کار من بیچاره قوی بسته شده
بگشای خدایا که گشاینده تویی

312

You are the redeemer of my ties;
      You are beyond any argument.
I've sufficient wealth that I am Your slave;
      I've sufficient glory that you are God.

313

You're God, aware of my heart;
      I'm helpless, You, the light of life.
An ant breathes at the bottom of a well,
      You, aware of the breath in that well.

314

You, the only eternal God,
      giver of morning from the skirt of night.
My affairs, O God, are tangled such:
      unravel my tangles, O Giver of light.

Notes to Poems

[1] A reference to the blinding light of God that appeared to Moses on the top of Mount Sinai. Even in the Old Testament the symbolism is not lost that there is an unbridgeable chasm between the Creator and the created.

[2] The Moslem shrine in Mecca toward which the faithful turn to pray. It is the "House of God," a black stone in the middle of a courtyard, signifying the Residence.

[3] Any capitalized reference is to God, especially the terms Friend and Lover, although, at times, the sacred and the secular run parallel.

[4] The Persian metaphor for "moth" is "butterfly." I have used the English idiom, which does not change the meaning but is more familiar.

[5] In Islam, for a divorce to be irrevocable, the man must pronounce his intentions three times.

[6] The words in Persian are *taráneh* and *kachul*, roughly in English "song, melody" and "*nux vomica*." Some sources use the combination with a coordinating conjunction *va*, which I translate as "joke and poison." Others omit *va*. In this case, "poison" becomes an adjective describing "song"; thus, "poisonous song."

[7] The original Persian text reads *bar bandeh-yeh bi-navá navái be-ferest*, which correctly could be translated as "to your indigent slaves send sustenance." However, this half-line could also be read as I have translated it. The word *navá* means both "a melody" and "sustenance." Lexically, the prefix *bi-* indicates a "lack of," so that *bi-navá* can be read as "without melody, songless" and also "indigent." I like the metaphor of music, and I have a feeling that Abu Sa'id may have had that in mind!

[8] This is one of many examples of Abu Sa'id's poetry in which the sacred and the secular exist side by side. This poem could be read as a love song to a woman or an invocation to the Creator by simply interpreting "you" as flesh or transcendental.

[9] In backgammon, winning is decided by reducing the number of tokens on the board; thus the pun on life, "winning is losing."

[10] Abu Sa'id uses two Koranic words, *salsabil* and *kowsar*, referring to a fountain and a river in the Garden of Eden. In Kowsar runs a river of milk and honey. My translation is a loose reference to these two words.

[11] From the modern Greek *zonári*. In early Islam, Nazarene Christians were ordered to wear a cloth over their garment, signifying that they were not Moslems, as the Jews were required to wear a patch of yellow cloth. Obviously, in his sense of fairness and tolerance, Abu Sa'id is juxtaposing that idea with his own that in

Love, insignificant signs do not matter, as *zonár* becomes an excessive symbol of Love.

[12] Abu Sa'id uses the word *mohtaseb*, literally a policeman, but in effect a low-ranking official with uncontrolled power to harass the citizens, a kind of Gestapo. "Censor" is the best I could translate this word.

[13] In most traditions, including Persian folklore, the salamander is thought to be able to live in fire without being consumed. In this line, the poet uses the hyperbole to show the intensity of the burning fire inside him that pours out as tears, carrying salamanders as a fire extinguisher.

[14] Abu Sa'id uses the metaphor of "face." However, since in the first half of the line I have used the word, I have translated *ruy* as "eyes," which is logical.

[15] Here is a wonderful juxtaposition of senses and sensations, which gives an elegant twist to the problem of hypocrisy: to see sound and hear action.

[16] Majnun is the mythological and literary Persian lover, who was in love with Leili, much celebrated and mentioned by a number of classical Persian poets, including Nezami, Hafez, and Rumi. His love was doomed, and he died a crazed man. In this quatrain Abu Sa'id plays with the word *jonun*, meaning "madness." In the first half of the second line the poet says, "I was the one who was chained for my madness," and in the second half he uses the name *Majnun*, "crazed," as a proper noun. The allusion is not lost for a Persian reader. This kind of juxtaposition is very common in Persian poetry and oral vernacular.

[17] The word in the poem is *dayr*, variously translatable to "monastery," "tavern," and "the world." All three meanings are present in the quatrain, and not a single English word can reveal these gradations of meaning. I have chosen "tavern" because on the literal level wine readily connects to it. However, on the metaphorical level, since the Sufi concept of the world is that of a tavern, an intimate place similar to a monastery, where the initiates gather, the reader might keep all these meanings in mind.

[18] Generally, the word *rend* (-*án*, pl.) characterizes a person with low morality and of the lowest caste in the society, the butt of the jokes of the higher, refined, spiritual and intellectual superiors. In Sufism the meaning is switched, and it relates *rend* to a person who is an irreverent free-thinker. He is irreligious but has a great sense of the divine. He is gruff and irrational outwardly but is filled with sensitivity and kindness inside. He disparages the cleric, but he has a sense of the presence of God. If the cleric is hypocritical, he is an honest man; a libertine and an honest man, trustworthy. A *rend* possesses equilibrium and lives according to the golden rule. This juxtaposition provides a Sufi with an even sharper tongue to criticize the ruling caste of the society and the cleric on their own terms.

[19] Abu Sa'id uses the word *pargár* (a pair of compasses), which has layers of cultural meaning in Persian. I have used "brush" as a substitute.

[20] The original line uses the word *chang*, referring ambiguously to "clutching, holding" and to "a harp." The literal meaning should read, "In the harp [clutches] of your sorrows my heart cannot sing melodies." I had to modify this translation because I could not find a word that could convey this ambiguity in English.

[21] See Note 18.

[22] The poet uses the Persian word *mojarrad* to imply—in a double entendre—both a unique entity and a person of experience, knowledge.

[23] It is interesting that Abu Sa'id, almost nine hundred years ago, talked about the transference theory of modern psychology, that is, what we see in others is only a reflection of ourselves, projected on them.

[24] Obviously, the poem should be read both on physical and metaphysical levels. Abu Sa'id's theology puts the onus on God for salvation: He argues that since God has created us and shown His face directly to us, there is no escaping that a love affair is going on between the Creator and the creature and that salvation is at hand because of this universal, uninterrupted, unimpeachable love. Please see the next poem, in which the idea is more boldly stressed.

[25] Khotan, famous for the high quality of its musk, is a city in Turkistan, now a part of China.

[26] An old measuring unit, slightly longer than 42 inches.

[27] This special use of the word refers to a shroud, a seamless piece of cotton cloth wrapped around the corpse before burial. The implication here is that before one starts the journey of life, one had better realize that one's main clothing is a shroud; spelled *kaftan*, it may also refer to a full-length garment with elbow-length or long sleeves, worn chiefly in eastern Mediterranean countries.

[28] Abu Sa'id plays with the word *come* in the last two half-lines. The literal translation is "He who that has come, it is beautiful. Know you that he who is caused to come [is brought] is not like the one who comes on his own."

[29] The sentiments expressed in this fatalistic poem are echoed in at least two of Omar Khayyám's quatrains. One wonders if the sentiments are medieval archetypes, used by many poets, or if Khayyám had read Abu Sa'id and was echoing him. The two quatrains are quoted below:

> This ocean of existence, appearing from concealment:
>> no one has ever unraveled its mysterious containment.
> Each to each has said a word or two in a manner, but
>> none has been able to reveal its secrets with contentment.

or

> Of all the travelers of this long journey—
>> who has returned to tell us the secrets of life?
> Then, in this crossroads of woes and sighs
>> you will not tarry nor will you ever return.

[30] The word "slain" does not carry the full import of Abu Sa'id's intentions. Quicksilver will remain unstable until it is mixed in an amalgam, when it loses its nature, but then again, it is no longer mercury. A lover must die in his beloved to lose his identity and acquire a different nature, thus losing his desolate, unstable state of being. This statement is remarkably Jungian and close to the Old Testament notion that "dying" means "having intercourse." Taken as a love song, the quatrain simply suggests that a lover will not be comfortable and happy until he consummates his love, literally, "sums up" with the lover. On the transcendental level—the Sufi's vision—as a lover of God, the individual is unfulfilled and unstable until he yields to the divine will and loses his own mundane nature. The metaphor of marriage between God and man is not a new one. Many western mystics—notably Julian of Norwich—have used it in describing those who wait for the Groom, Jesus, to rescue the bride from the travails of life through a marriage. Catholic nuns, when taking their vows, give their hands to Christ as a bride, but in doing so, they deny their earthly nature.

[31] In the Islamic tradition, a dog is unclean, although it also is a working friend. If a dog is touched, an ablution is required. The metaphor sets the meaning of the first two half-lines in focus. It is the nature of the elements that should be considered, and an uncorrupted element—the ocean—cannot be corrupted by a corrupt nature (dog). Thus, when a person has an inner light, he glows on his own and has no need of light from the outside of the self.

[32] Juniper is a traditional metaphor for the beautiful, slim, and tall body of the beloved. The word often crops up in Hafez, Omar Khayyám, and Rumi.

[33] The word Abu Sa'id uses is *khájeh*, which, strictly speaking, translates to "man of distinction."

[34] The word used here is *saháb*, roughly, "a nebula." I have translated it as "cloud" for convenience.

[35] A Persian mythical creature, generally resembling a lizard, believed capable of living in or withstanding fire.

[36] The metaphors of "thorn" and "path" are distinctly medieval Persian. However, in modern English they should make sense, thorn referring to forbearance of suffering and path referring to hardship of traveling on foot. In the conceit, the poet says that the thought of the beloved has transformed the hard road and thorn into a flower garden, such is the intensity of his love. There is an interesting parallelism

here with the passion of Christ, when a crown of thorns is put on his head. He bears it for the love of his Father and humankind.

[37] The metaphor of "tear" paints a wonderful image of drawing on the shifting water, like painting on the impermanent sand.

[38] "Sexton" alludes to the Christian religion and "prayer rug" to Islam. Abu Sa'id seems to treat religions equally, especially with the harsh reference to *zonár* in the last line; zonár was a cummerbund worn by the Eastern Nestorian Christians and the Jews by the order of the Moslem rulers to distinguish them from the Moslems: a worthless piece of cloth, Abu Sa'id says. The import of the poem seems to be that only human souls matter, and the vestments of organized religions, unless they totally address human soul, are worldly and subject to scorn if abused.

[39] "Giver-and-breaker" in this line refers to God, from whom everything flows, and He is the final arbiter of affairs, good or bad. Here, Abu Sa'id is echoing the Sufi stance that everything is of the divine providence, including evil, which human beings do not understand or misinterpret. Abu Sa'id is saying, "Thy will be done...."

[40] Here is a play on the word *license*. In line three, the word means "permission," and in line four it is "deviation from truth." Both definitions are in *The American Heritage Dictionary,* among others.

[41] I assume "both worlds" refers to this world and the one to come.

[42] Nowruz (The New Day) is the first day of the year in the Persian calendar. It coincides with the first day of spring, normally the 21st of March. Nowruz is more than just a day; older calculations—confirmed by modern mathematics—pinpoint the exact time the earth starts a new revolution around the sun, and that moment—*tahvil*—is both sacred and secular. Celebrations go on for thirteen days.

[43] This delicate play with the word *tulip* creates a visual imagery: tulip normally looks up, to the heavens, until it has lost its freshness and is dying, at which time it turns upside down (bowing the head), creating a bell. Juxtaposed with the sound that the caravan of time in Nowruz should make but does not until the tulip is dying, the imagery becomes a melancholic expression of sad dejection and confirmation of the poet's state of mind expressed in the second line.

[44] I think this is an echo of the Sufi value that man is redeemed by God through grace, not works. Abu Sa'id is emboldened to "guarantee" redemption by availing himself to accept everyone's sin, exactly what Christ did by offering himself as a sacrificial lamb for the sins of the world—for the redemption of man. This will be echoed two centuries later by Hafez as "The Mercy of God is greater than my sins...."

[45] Formerly known as the Oxus, a river of central Asia flowing generally northwest along much of the Turkistan–Afghanistan border to the southern Aral Sea. In this sense, the poet uses the hyperbole of abundance of tears to juxtapose the lover's place and the natural reservoir of water in the eyes!

[46] In English, it is an almost incomprehensible poem and poetic phrasing; in Persian, it expresses an enigma, rather than a cogent poetic thought. Abu Sa'id uses Persian grammatical terms to construct his enigma. *'yen* and *zât* [glottal stop and voiced interdental fricative] are names for two graphemes in the Persian/Arabic alphabet, but both also have a lexical meaning: "nature," "substance," "intrinsic essence." In the first line Abu Sa'id uses the word *khat*, meaning a line, but in combination it also means "to cancel out, to disregard." And, in the first part of line three he uses *jomleh*, meaning a sentence but also "all, a sum." Through double entendre, the poet writes a perfectly delightful poem in Persian, but in English? I have included this quatrain for explanatory reasons in the introduction to show that no matter how a translator tries to be faithful to a text, there comes a time when he must simply gloss over the original and rewrite the intentions of the original text, thus abolishing it and creating something that is not really related to the original text.

[47] The word, perhaps from *Frank* or *Frankish*, referring to the French, has been used in Iran to denote any European.

[48] The word Abu Sa'id uses should be translated as "sorrows"; however, "yearn" fits better with the general meaning of the poem.

[49] Reference is to the "Wheel of Fortune."

[50] An ironic tone gives a light touch to this poem. In the traditional Persian property laws, every parcel is divided into six parts called *dángs*, regardless of the size of the property. Owning a *dáng* was a hassle because others owned the rest. One had to own all six *dángs* to call the property one's own. Abu Sa'id jokes that not only he owns only one part, even "a whit less." With the same ironic tone the poet talks of buying two jugs of wine, but "a dram less." Then, his harp does not play sharp or base notes: here is a world where nothing is "full" and complete, yet his friend talks of lovesickness and *ghalandari*!

[51] *Ghalandar* and *rend* both refer to people who are rebels and who follow an unorthodox path of faith. At the time Abu Sa'id wrote, the terms were pejorative, although four centuries later, Hafez cleansed them and made the terms stand for the highest level of spirituality. For a detailed discussion, please see Reza Ordoubadian, *The Ghazals of Hafez* (Ibex, 2003).

[52] A tree with sweet, fragrant wood, used to scent an area.

[53] The original text of the line reads, "My face has become black and my hair white." This does not make sense in English and may even have racial overtones. I think the biblical "ashes and sackcloth" is the intention of the poet.

[54] The word can be more literally translated as "hopelessness, dejection, lack of hope." I have used, instead, the word *dream*, which incorporates at once both a falseness and also hope and positive feelings.

[55] To extract rose essence for rose water, bundles of fresh rose flowers are distilled over a very hot fire. The metaphor here is the word *smile,* which refers to the short life of human beings in this world.

[56] In a wonderful juxtaposition of two words in Persian, Abu Sa'id creates his second line by the use of the homophonous words *khoshk* and *tar*, meaning "dry" and "wet." In the first half he uses the words in their literal level: parched lips and dampened eyes; however, in the second half, when the two Persian words are combined, he gets what I have translated as "of all the wealth…," or "of all the dry things and wet things in the universe." I wish this could be reproduced to show the play on words and sounds, but I am not able to find a way of relating it except in an explanatory footnote. The transliteration of the second line follows:

> dáram lab **khoshk** o dideh **tar** bepazir/
> I have **dry** lip and **wet** eye, accept.
>
> kaz **khoshk** o **tare** jahán hamin dáram/
> For, of the **dry** and **wet** of the world this is all I have.

[57] Again, here we have a translator's hell! Abu Sa'id uses the word *nár* which can mean "hell," or "do not bring, not breathe out," or "pomegranate"; thus, the allusion to "blood." The word is repeated four times at the end of each half-line with a different meaning in mind. It is one thing to find meaningful words for each usage in English, but they hardly convey the playful tone that the poet gives to his poem by his masterful manipulation of these homophonous words. The total effect of the music of the poem partially depends on the rhyme that these words create.

[58] Wine bearer, usually a young boy.

[59] This apparently simple poem is very complex. There are a number of possible interpretations: (1) death is inevitable; (2) life is transitory; (3) there is a difference between the speaker of the poem and other people, since others die when their cup is full (a clever allusion to "cup runneth over") but the speaker dies when the cup is empty. Yet in the difference lies in the similarity: all die, no matter if the cup is full or empty. In this sense, Saghi becomes a symbol of the divine fate and the destiny. The interesting point in the poem is in its juxtaposing "full" and "empty." When a cup is full, there is nothing left and death comes; when the cup is empty, there is no sustenance left, and death comes, death, that equalizer of the living.

[60] I presume the reference is to the Judgment of God before eternity.

[61] Narcissus is a symbol for beautiful eyes, bedroom eyes.

[62] The Koran promises Moslems the reward of Paradise and a river that runs through it, the Kosar. What flows through it is "sweeter than honey, whiter than milk, colder than snow, and softer than cream" [*al Kowsar S*, The Koran].

[63] In the Koranic tradition, Khezr is a companion of Moses, and is full of tricks. He has a special position with Sufis, equal to "Pir-e Moghán" or Master, as I have translated it here. Perhaps the reference is to the Old Testament Elias/Elijah, who did not die but ascended to heaven and has eternal life [Old Testament, Kings I and II].

[64] This is a play on words: life/Life. The word in lowercase refers to the voice in the poem, his life. With the capital letter it refers to his beloved, who is more dear to him than his own life and, perhaps, God.

[65] Compare these lines with the following lines from John Donne's "A Valediction Forbidding Mourning" (A.D. 1572–1632):

> If they be two, they are two so
> > As stiff twin compasses are two.
> Thy soul, the fixed foot, makes no show
> > To move, but doth, if the other do.

Also, compare them with the lines in Nos. 85 and 88 of Hafez (A.D. 1325–1389) in Ordoubadian, *The Poems of Hafez*, published by Ibex in 2003:

Like a pair of compasses, my heart roves in all directions:

yet in the circling it remains an erect rover.

> The sage are the fixéd point of a pair of compasses,

> > yet Love knows: they are lost—in their circle!

[66] The allusion is to the skin that covers a tambourine: thin, responsive, and a slave to the musician and his whims. The phrase "skin wearer" could be taken as "naked, without possibilities," as in born naked and without worldly goods: also, the poor used animal skins to protect themselves against the elements.

[67] The frame of a tambourine is fitted with numerous bells and jingles to sound as the musician desires. "Ring in the ear" is an idiom referring to a slave.

[68] The last two lines indicate the total obedience of the lover in the court of the beloved. The beloved's words are *farmans* (edicts) of the ruler to be obeyed without question.

[69] A dervish is the Moslem equivalent of a monk or friar; the Persian word dár-vish is the ultimate source of dervish, meaning a "religious mendicant." Of the

qualities of a dervish, simplicity, vow of poverty, and selflessness are the most prized. There were, of course, men who wore dervish clothing only for self-gain and pretense, an act considered the height of arrogance and ná-darvishi (lack of the qualities of a dervish) by Hafez.

[70] The word used is *mestaba*, or a stone bench erected in a tavern, upon which men sat and drank their wine.

[71] In a tragic Persian and Arabic legend, similar to that of Romeo and Juliet, Leili and Majnun, two members of the same tribe, grow up together and finally fall in love. Majnun's father would not consent to their marriage, Majnun goes mad, and the lovers die of heartbreak. Majnun literally means "a crazed person, a person who has lost his mind because of unrequited love."

[72] Abu Sa'id uses the word "crystal ball," which has the symbolic meaning of seeing the universe for an insightful understanding of the purpose of creation. I think that the "I" is representative of "We," the creatures. If one were to look into the heart of one individual being with discerning eyes, one might be able to understand the purpose of the "Sultan," the Creator; thus, one can find God's purpose in *the other*.

[73] *ná-* is negation here, literally meaning "he is no Dervish at all."

[74] In this poem, highly structured with a complex use of the words *swell* and *Ocean*—both with and without capital O—the poet sets out to express one of his metaphysical statements. The Ocean is a reference to God and swell to a limited manifestation of God. As a watcher of waves sees only the swell and not the source—Ocean—itself, so does man see only a swell of God's being and not God. From the "interior" of the ocean the watcher observes the surface of the swell, but in that swell is hidden the ocean that is not apparent to the eye, thus a mystery. I suggest that this is a Sufi's allusion to man who is in God and God who is in man.

[75] Attendance.

[76] The word used by the poet is *tambourine*, referring to the roundness of their faces with, perhaps, long earrings, reminiscent of the bells on a tambourine. I have changed it to "moon-faces" for poetic reasons.

[77] The line could be literally translated as "So long as the perfect light illuminates the sun, its source remains invisible." In other words, one cannot look into the sun directly without a filter, a mask, to keep the dazzling light from blinding one's eye.

[78] In translation some idioms had to be compromised. In Persian, "to reach to the skirt" of someone means "to have a connection, to ask for help." In the poem Abu Sa'id plays on this idiom; the literal translation might help here: "It does not profit

for you to stay at home. I must tie your skirt to my skirt. The day my hand is on your skirt, we cannot sever from your skirt." The philosophical content deals with the idea of living in isolation or in a community. So long as we have the "skirt" of another held in our hands, we continue living fruitfully in a community. Please refer to the introduction for a concept of mortification and insular living, as Abu Sa'id practiced in his early youth.

[79] The word is a reference to France and the French, who apparently first came in contact with the Iranians. However, it refers generally to non-Moslem, Christian foreigners of the west.

[80] The Moslem shrine toward which the faithful turn to pray and make pilgrimage.

[81] A reference to the Joseph of the Old Testament; Joseph's beauty mesmerized women and men alike. In the Koran a beautiful love story is told of Joseph and Zuleikha.

[82] "Honey" could be taken as a love potion of supreme potency, a sheer physical intoxication, or it could be a reference to the metaphysical, transcendent nectar to reach the Creator. This is a good example of a poem with a parallel deep structure, where both the physical and the spiritual weave through. The word *spit* has a double meaning: "spit at me, who is giving you the honey, as a gesture of disappointment," or "spit it out if you don't like it, but I know you will like it."

[83] Abu Sa'id toys with words in this poem. The import of the quatrain is that the lover's whispering a secret at night will not necessarily hold in the daylight. He uses words for garments to explain it. The secret at night, when verbalized, will not be covered as if a shirt is worn over the secret, because as one pulls a shirt over one's head, the collar may be too tight for the head to go through. Then, the poet reiterates by saying, the shirt of words has a tight skirt, hard to wear. In other words, a secret once whispered—even privately in a lover's bed—cannot remain a secret for long.

[84] Oxus River, otherwise known as Amu Darya. The Oxus starts from the Pamir Mountains and empties into both the Caspian Sea and the Aral Sea.

[85] Refers to Mount Caucasus, which, according to Persian lore, surrounds the world. This is the same mountain on which, according to Greek lore, Prometheus was bound.

[86] Abu Sa'id uses several of the many idioms possible with the Persian word *sar*, "head," to construct a playful two lines, especially the second half of the second line. This translation is a remoter rendition of what the poet writes, but the meaning and his intent are kept intact.

[87] The Moslem shrine toward which the faithful turn to pray.

[88] *Ghabá* is a long garment open in the front, and worn by men. Hat and ghabá are the simple, unostentatious, traditional wear used commonly. The advice is that "heart," the inner garment, is more important in wooing a lover (perhaps, God) than is trying to put on modish garb.

[89] The original line reads, "Better wear black garment when people wear many colored garments." This is an idiom that directs the reader to "wear black" (hide), when "people wear many colored garments" (they are pretentious).

[90] This line in Abu Sa'id reads, "I fear that from fear and hope, all things said and done, the person who has done will be taken as a person who has not, and the person who has not done, as a person who has." In other words, the sinner will be redeemed and the virtuous not; this is akin to what Jesus says, "...[I]t is easier for a camel to go through the eye of a needle than for a rich man to enter the kingdom of God" [Matthew 19:24].

[91] "King of Twain Worlds" and "The Lion of God" both refer to Ali, the cousin of Prophet Mohammad and his son-in-law, who became the first imam for the Shiites. That Abu Sa'id, a Shafi Sunni, uses the terms in the context is an indication of his supreme respect for religions and sects different from his own.

[92] In Iranian mythology, the phoenix is a symbol of wisdom and high-mindedness.

[93] The first line in Persian reads, "You have etched your face in all our houses," which does not make sense in English. The metaphor should be "heart."

[94] "Tulip," an alternative term for "rose," is traditional imagery for describing a beautiful face, a lover's face.

[95] There is no such a word in any English dictionary; I have made it up from the word "heathen" for my special needs in the poem.

[96] When in the course of a day Moslems pray, they momentarily put their heads on the ground on a piece of clay-cube, *mohr* —from a holy place—as a sign of yielding and resignation.

[97] In a tragic Persian and Arabic legend, close to that of Romeo and Juliet, Leili and Majnun, two members of the same tribe, grow up together and finally fall in love. Majnun's father does not consent to their marriage, and the lovers die of heartbreak. The reference to Zuleikha here is to Potiphar's wife, who, according to the Koran, tried to seduce Joseph. The Islamic version is a full short story, delicately fashioned and poetically told. Many Persian poets refer to these two sets of possible lovers to allude to unrequited, impossible love.

[98] According to the Islamic tradition, on the day of resurrection the sun and the moon will rise at the same time, but from opposite directions. Here, the poet

compares the light of the daybreak with the light emanating from the lover's face, both unveiled.

99 Throwing a victim in a well was considered in the courts as a just punishment and was common. In the traditional Islamic world, clapping hands was a sign of summoning and ordering, and thus a signal for carrying out the command of drowning. This is one of very few political poems Abu Sa'id ever wrote.

100 Raising the hand to the heart refers to a symbolic gesture that means the act of killing comes from the heart, as a duty. It could also mean that despite the act and the murderous order, the sultan still has some kindly feelings toward the victim. This explanation and the one in Note 93 are suggestions of Shahriar Zangeneh.

101 Ecclesiastic or moral police, who patrolled the city streets to arrest and jail those who behaved outside Islamic laws.

102 The Moslem shrine toward which the faithful turn to pray and make pilgrimage.

103 The word God is only implicit in the poem.

104 As in the west, white hair is a sign of honor and wisdom that comes with age. Black, in contrast, is a symbol of disgrace and shame.

105 The idiom "on my eyes" is the highest honor one can give any person as superior. This is a statement of acquiescence and submission.

106 The metaphor alludes to men of greatness who battle in important fields; that is, at the time one cannot find any man to measure up to the ideal, a man who will unselfishly do great deeds for the world, a true hero.

107 In the original poem, the poet plays on the many meanings of the Persian word *beh*. As it variously means a "quince," "better," "bravo," and "well done," it is impossible to find homophonous words that would convey these different meanings.

Bibliography

Dámádi, Mohammad. *Abu Sa'id Nameh*. Tehran: University of Tehran Press, 1995. (Persian text).
A short discussion of the station of Abu Sa'id and his position in the Sufi thought of Iran, the book contains numerous charts and indexes.

Jamaleddin Abu Ruh Lotfollah. *Hálát va Sokhanán-e Sheykh Abu Sa'id Abul-Kheyr Miháneh* [The State of Grace and Words of Sheikh Abu Sa'id Abul-Kheyr], written by 1147 C.E., first published in St. Petersburg, Russia, by Valentin Zhukovskiy in 1899. Edited, corrected with notes and explanations by Mohammad-Reza Shafi'i Kadkani, Tehran: Agah Press, 1995. (Persian text)

Meir, Fritz. *Abu Sa'id-i Abi'l-Hayr 357-440/967-1049. Wirklichkeit und Legende.* Translated with a compendium of notes and indexes by Professor Mehr Afagh Beybordi. Tehran: Iran University Press, 1378/1999. (Persian text used)

Mohammad Nureddin Monavvar bin Abi Sa'id. *Asrar at-Towhid fi Maghamat-e Sheikh Abi Sa'id (Secrets of Oneness [Monotheism] in the Sermons of Sheikh Abu Sa'id). 1178, 1192 C.E..* First published in St. Petersburg, Russia, by Valentin Zhukovskiy in 1899. The manuscript is in the British Museum under the Codex No. Or. 249. (Persian text)

Ordoubadian, Reza. *The Poems of Hafez.* Bethesda, MD: Ibex Publishers, 2006. (English text)

Poetry of Abu Sa'id Abu Kheyr. Collected, edited, authenticated with notes and indexes by Sa'id Nafisi. Sixth edition. Tehran: Sana'i Publishers, 1995. (Persian text)

Rubaiyat-e Abu Sa'id Abi'l -Kheyr. Edited by Saber Kermáni. Tehran: Eqbal Publishers, 1991. (Persian text)

Rubaiyat-e Abu Sa'id Abol Kheyr, Khayyam, [and] Bábá Táher. Corrected and edited by Jahangir Mansuri. Tehran: Nahid Publishers, 1996. (Persian text)

Zangeneh, Shahriar, e-mail text, January 2003.

Index to First Lines

Other Titles of Interest from Ibex Publishes